World-Forming and Contemporary Art

I0474431

This book explores how contemporary art can alter the ways in which we visualise and conceptualise the world and the social relations that shape it. Drawing from the writings of philosopher Jean-Luc Nancy, it spotlights the concept of 'world-forming' and the political significance of art-making and viewing.

The central theme of 'world-forming' focuses attention on the processes of globalisation. The book explores how artists can facilitate shared creative spaces within and beyond the apparatuses of global capitalism. The book traces a philosophical progression from ontology to the political through a series of participatory practices. It forwards Jean-Luc Nancy's idea of 'world-forming' in order to show how contemporary art sustains critical and creative engagement with social practices. The overall objective of the book is to show, through participatory practices, how contemporary art can facilitate social change.

The book will be of interest to scholars working in art history, contemporary art, philosophy and politics.

Jessica Holtaway is Lecturer at Solent University. Her research centres on politically-engaged artworks and performances.

Routledge Focus on Art History and Visual Studies

World-Forming and Contemporary Art

Jessica Holtaway

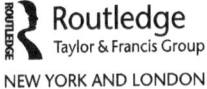 Routledge
Taylor & Francis Group

NEW YORK AND LONDON

First published 2021
by Routledge
605 Third Avenue, New York, NY 10017

and by Routledge
2 Park Square, Milton Park, Abingdon, Oxon, OX14 4RN

Routledge is an imprint of the Taylor & Francis Group, an informa business

Library of Congress Cataloging-in-Publication Data
Names: Holtaway, Jessica, author.
Title: World-forming and contemporary art / Jessica Holtaway.
Description: New York : Routledge, 2021. | Includes
    bibliographical references and index.
Identifiers: LCCN 2020040492 (print) | LCCN 2020040493
    (ebook) | ISBN 9780367628390 (hardback) | ISBN
    9781003111023 (ebook)
Subjects: LCSH: Art, Modern—21st century—Philosophy. | Art
    and globalization—History—21st century. | Art and society—
    History—21st century. | Nancy, Jean-Luc.
Classification: LCC N6497 .H65 2021 (print) | LCC N6497
    (ebook) | DDC 709.05—dc23
LC record available at https://lccn.loc.gov/2020040492
LC ebook record available at https://lccn.loc.gov/2020040493

ISBN 13: 978-0-367-62839-0 (hbk)

Typeset in Times New Roman
by Apex CoVantage, LLC

Contents

Figures

Acknowledgements

I would like to express my great appreciation to Dr. Jean-Paul Martinon for his attentive reading of early versions of this book. I would also like to thank Professor John Paul Ricco, Dr. Robert Luzar and Dr. Nicola Foster, whose insights and questions helped me sharpen my analysis.

I am grateful to fellow members of Liberate Tate for inspiring conversations and for reminding me of the contemporary urgency of radical institutional critique.

I would like to thank Kaori Homma, Meryl Doney and Dr. Yoshitaka Mōri from Art Action UK, who gave thoughtful feedback on my analyses of our projects and facilitated the development of particular themes within our programme of events.

I thank Gaia Rosenberg-Colorni from Arnolfini for sharing knowledge and research about the Arts Council England's Quality Metrics pilot.

The friendship and dynamism of my fellow researchers in PLANK (Politically-Led Art and Networked Knowledge) has been invaluable to me. Dr. Paula Serafini, Dr. Alberto Cossu and Dr. Marc Herbst have each impacted my thinking and approach to both academia and activism.

Finally, I would like to thank my friends and family for their steadfast support and encouragement throughout my research.

Abbreviations

The following abbreviations are used to refer to key texts by Jean-Luc Nancy:

IC	*The Inoperative Community* (1991)
WCATS	*Who Comes After the Subject* (1991)
BtP	*The Birth to Presence* (1993)
M	*The Muses* (1996)
SoW	*The Sense of the World* (1997)
RtP	*Retreating the Political (Nancy & Philippe Lacoue-Labarthe)* (1997)
BSP	*Being Singular Plural* (2000)
GoI	*The Ground of the Image* (2005)
MA	*Multiple Arts: The Muses II* (2006)
CoW	*The Creation of the World or Globalization* (2007)
D	*Dis-Enclosure: The Deconstruction of Christianity* (2008)
AF	*After Fukushima: The Equivalence of Catastrophes* (2015)
DC	*The Disavowed Community* (2016)

Introduction

> Our task today is nothing less than the task of creating a form or a symbolization of the world. This seems to us to be the greatest risk that humanity has had to confront. . . . It is the extremely concrete and determined task – a task that can only be a struggle – of posing the following question to each gesture, each conduct, each habitus and each ethos: How do you engage the world? How do you involve yourself with the enjoyment of the world as such, and not with the appropriation of a quantity of equivalence?
>
> (Jean-Luc Nancy: *The Creation of the World or Globalization*: 2007c: 53)

The task of creating a 'form' or 'symbolisation' of the world feels more complex than ever before. Sudden limits in mobility and social interaction, following the worldwide Covid-19 pandemic, have led to decisive political actions and required the majority of the world's population to alter consumption habits and social behaviour. Mainstream media outlets have begun to discuss the end of capitalism. Beyond the immediacy of responding to a pandemic, we are increasingly aware that ecological crises are intensifying. Facing the gravity of these contemporary issues, cultural practices such as art could be understood as simple distractions, ineffectual and even indulgent. However, this book argues that art provokes us to question our understanding of the world, providing a vital critical lens on the networks and hierarchies of power that characterise and reinforce 'global capitalism'.[1]

This book spotlights the importance of 'recomposing' the image of the world. It explores how creative practices can sustain a critical and formative role in the way in which we constitute our environments. Although creative practices are constantly at risk of absorption into reductive systems of exchange, often unreliable in their ability to communicate a clear-cut sense of the world, they nevertheless have a vanguard role in campaigns for social change. Turning to philosopher Jean-Luc Nancy, this study takes the concept of 'world-forming' as an entry point into this central question: How can contemporary art help us to recompose the image of the world, and why is this significant?

To focus this question, I work with Nancy's philosophical study of being – his ontology – through three cultural practices: performances with the art group Liberate Tate (a London-based collective that focuses on ending oil sponsorship of the arts, in particular BP's sponsorship of the Tate), curatorial practices with an arts collective, Art Action UK (who provide an annual residency for artists who live and work in Japan and are responding to the nuclear disaster of 2011) and educational practices with a contemporary arts institution, the Arnolfini in Bristol. As such, I analyse a trajectory in the practice of 'recomposing' images, from the ontology of emergent creative practices, through to the role of curators as agents in creating a new 'sense' of the world, to look at how micro-political processes of transformation are structurally played out within larger cultural institutions.

In *The Creation of the World*, Nancy explains how 'worldhood' is 'never inscribed in a representation, and nonetheless always at work and in circulation in the forms that are being invented' (2007c: 52). He critiques terms such as 'worldview', explaining that a represented world is 'dependant on the gaze of the subject of the world', who cannot be in the world (2007c: 40). This study explores how, by following Nancy's philosophy of being, we can relinquish the idea of 'the subject'. Consequently, it explores how the process of 'recomposing the image of the world' allows us to understand how the world can never be fully represented (or 'inscribed in a representation'). For Nancy, art 'disengages the world from signification' (M 1996: 22). Here art plays a paradoxical role in our understanding of the world, because although it requires images, these images serve to interrupt, expose and challenge our 'worldview', heightening the sense of shared separation that constitutes being and being-with the world.

Contemporary theorists have addressed the 'destruction of the image of the globe' (Latour 2013) and called for us to 'recapitulate' what globalisation means (Berger 2016). This book puts forward the term 'recomposing'. To 'recompose' – to compose again or differently – carries a sense of a shared process (*com*) of withdrawing, distancing or undoing (*re-*) that *poses* a question whilst 'suggesting' or 'placing' a new image (only to facilitate a further withdrawal). This term is interpreted in the context of Nancy's writings and is explored through the development of these three cultural practices.

I have undertaken a study of three specific concepts within Nancy's writings – spacing, exscribing and co-appearing. This study has been practice-based – research has been undertaken through art performances, curatorial practice[2] and institutional research. It is therefore an 'embodied' reading of Nancy, with the aim of exploring the concrete significance of his writings. This book follows the creative flux of art practices and identifies points throughout this evolution where such practices risk absorption into capitalist apparatuses of power and knowledge. Finally, it analyses ways in which creative practices can facilitate a critical awareness of, and possibly retreat from, these apparatuses.

I start with the hypothesis that to 'recompose' the image of the world requires critical engagement with prevailing conceptual frameworks, engagement that develops through a process of distancing from dominant paradigms of knowledge. To test this hypothesis, I draw from the philosophical readings of Nancy and develop a discursive analysis of his writings along with texts by Georges Bataille, Paulo Virno, Maurice Blanchot, Carl Schmitt and Hannah Arendt. As my analysis evolves alongside participatory practices, the theoretical scope broadens from an initial close reading of Nancy's earlier texts, with their philosophical focus on ontology, to wider discussions that draw from political theory. Although this theoretical scope is admittedly rather Eurocentric, I hope that my reading of these thinkers opens up critical discussions and facilitates new readings and understandings of contemporary arts practice and political engagement.

This book ultimately addresses the meaning of 'the political' and what it means to be politically engaged today. Taking up Nancy's metaphor of theory as a 'slope' or 'inclination' (Morin 2012: 113 – referring to a colloquium conversation in 2002), I examine creative practices that appear as specific loci on the 'incline' from his philosophy of being through to the political. More specifically I start by looking at how one political art practice (the work of Liberate Tate) operates through communicative strategies that shape social zeitgeists in a contagious and contingent way. I explore ways in which freedom can be sustained through intentional strategies of engagement. The book then addresses the role of curatorial practices with reference to Art Action UK, situating curators in an ethical position, with the responsibility of sustaining freedom of expression and facilitating social engagement. Finally, I turn to the role of cultural institutions (in particular the Arnolfini in Bristol) and consider how institutions might respond to the conflicting demands of their publics, and of funding bodies.

Throughout the following pages, I aim to provide an active reflection on political art practices that can act as a resource for both practitioners and theorists. Theoretical discourses around art activism can, at times, mute or deactivate creative practices by reinforcing their role in achieving a particular end. However, through a series of evaluations of current discourses on political art, the book outlines and participates in processes of critical reflection that facilitate and advance the creative potential of art practices.

What Is at Stake in This Study?

As we continue our lives amidst the global Covid-19 pandemic, it is more important than ever to ask 'how do we engage the world?' (Nancy 2007c: 53) and to continue to recompose the image of the world. For Nancy, writing in April 2020 in the *European Journal of Psychoanalysis*, coronavirus is 'on every level, a product of globalisation' taking part in 'the wider process through which a culture becomes undone, to be replaced by something which is less a culture and more a system of forces indistinguishably technical, economic, authoritarian and sometimes psychological or physical' (13/4/2020). The same journal also published Nancy's response to Giorgio Agamben (originally published in Italian on 'Antinomie'), who suggests that governments have taken advantage of this global crisis, conceptualising it as an exception that validates further control and surveillance of populations (Agamben 26/02/2020). Writing again in the *European Journal of Psychoanalysis*, Agamben writes of his concern that as we live more of our lives online, machines begin to 'replace any contact – any contagion – between human beings' (17/03/2020). For Nancy, the Covid-19 pandemic shows us how exception is becoming the rule in a world of intensifying technological interconnections (27/02/2020). Nevertheless, in an article on Verso's website (27/03/20), he writes about how the pandemic is 'communizing us', equalising us in its necessity for a common stand, but that this experience of community is paradoxical – we have to be spatially distanced and isolated to care for others. For Nancy, it is now more important than ever to 'ask ourselves how far we can better understand the nature of our community' (Nancy on Verso 27/03/20).

This book focuses attention on the role of art in helping us understand the nature of our community. Since the 1960s, when contemporary art practices increasingly began to take place outside of the traditional museum space, and particularly in Europe and America, more people have begun to turn to socially engaged art practice[3] as a way of addressing micro-political issues. These practices often take the form of collaborative workshops, performances and interventions, in which the emphasis is on the process rather than on the final product[4]. This book has evolved from a critical evaluation of current theoretical approaches that often reduce such practices to determinative illustrations of politics or that reinforce differences between aesthetics and politics – approaches that continue to influence and inspire curatorial practices within cultural institutions. Contemporary theorists, notably Nicolas Bourriaud and Jacques Rancière, have sparked ongoing debates around the terms 'politics' and 'aesthetics'. Often, by addressing these terms, even in attempts to unify them, these debates tend to fortify a sense that 'aesthetics' – principles concerned with the nature of beauty – only 'lend' significance to political discourses (Rancière 2004: 19) which are (contrastingly) part of 'real' systems and social realities (Bourriaud 1998: 36). However, these theoretical discussions begin to point to a renewed perception of the political, a theme that is developed throughout the following chapters.

Art as a form of social critique is a familiar concept to most – artists and artworks have been agents of history, changing attitudes and provoking questions. In the last decade, this role has become central to many artistic discourses. But often, popular discourses focus on how creative practices illustrate a particular political idea, ignoring powerful nuances and failing to recognise ways in which artworks can recompose perceptions of politics and globalisation, and sustain a sense of creative freedom.

In recent years artists have been dismissed and marginalised, silenced and even imprisoned because of fears over the social impact of their work.[5] Ironically, in many cases, these works become amplified through attempts to censor them. Nevertheless, increased media coverage and acceptance within the 'art world' does not guarantee the sustained agency of such works. As outlined, academic discourses often gravitate towards debates around the relationship between art and politics, an assumed relationship between what are seen as separate sources of power. These assumptions reinforce processes of differentiation that immediately reduce the creative potential of the works in question. These discourses are explored in the first chapter. From prevailing desires to glean an immediate understanding of the meaning 'in' an artwork, to curatorial approaches that reinforce pedagogic narratives, and to institutions that use art as a tool for a wider set of aims tied up in funding and government policies, it is not surprising that creative processes are quickly appropriated and spaces for critical reflection diminished.

Why Nancy?

Jean-Luc Nancy, born in Cauderan, France in 1940, studied philosophy in Paris and wrote his doctoral dissertation on Kant. His subsequent writings have reflected on the writings of Marx, Nietzsche, Breton, Heidegger, Bataille, Blanchot and Derrida amongst others, situating him within the tradition of continental philosophy, with its exploration of psychoanalysis, deconstruction and critical theory. Responding to the writings of 'post-structuralists' (many of whom reject this categorisation), Nancy's texts embody a critical relationship to dominant ideological structures, highlighting the radical relationship between language and knowledge, and fragmenting perceptions of history as a totality. Within this lineage of thinking, Nancy approaches themes of globalisation, religion, art, culture, disease, community, sovereignty and many more – addressing philosophical ideas through analysis of unfolding events. It is Nancy's expansive critical approach – demonstrated through over 50 books and manifold articles, catalogue texts and interviews – that gives his writing a contemporary relevance and urgency. However, these writings, developed from a Kantian philosophy of finitude and through a deconstruction of Christianity, have brought Nancy's philosophies into question, especially through the writings of speculative materialists, such as Quentin Meillassoux.[6] Although these debates are not central to this book, I nevertheless advance a reading of Nancy's texts that might begin to address the alleged limits of Nancy's thought.

To read and apply texts by Nancy in the context of institutional practices may seem incongruent with his writings, which forward a philosophy of being that is pre-institutional. Nevertheless, the following analysis seeks to address the concrete significance of Nancy's thought, and suggest a renewed approach to the idea of 'the institutional'. In an interview in *Diacritics* in 2015, Nancy states, 'Sense can only be *in common* (exchange, sending, referring, sharing); it cannot be *common* (granted by a common institution or constitution, or by and as a common order)' (2015: 104). Being-in-common is prior to an institution, it is a kind of anarchy – the antithesis of institutionality. Nevertheless, at the centre of a *cultural* institution is a sense of art as a form of open-ended communication that has social importance (even as this becomes expressed in economic terms). A cultural institution is structured around such incommensurability and 'sense'. In the same interview Nancy states that 'politics must remain held in reserve for sense (*se tienne en réserve du sens*): it must be understood as being in the service of the community, rather than its principle and end' (2015: 104, 105). As will be considered, ethical issues arise when art institutions aim to be in the 'service of the community' by attempting to 'produce' or 'grant' sense rather than *allowing* the common to take place informally, beyond the institution. I am interested in how cultural institutions can sustain the possibility of informal sites of 'exchange, sending, referring, sharing' – how they can be 'in common' by actively refraining from processes of quantification. Similarly, when I consider the 'agency' of art, I am interested in agency as free choice – agency manifest through the decisions that shape conceptualisations of the world. Agency is not necessarily goal directed – creativity affirms a sense of open-ended agency.

The political importance of creativity is clearly emphasised by many contemporary cultural and political theorists. Visual media is a vital form of communication within capitalist strategies because it is capable of shaping conscious and subconscious aspirations. Creative practices can also be appropriated by political powers and wielded to terrifying effect. Nevertheless, art always brings with it a question, as well as an awareness of its speculative nature. Art can be used to coerce, but it is never entirely reducible to a straightforward function – it brings with it a shadow of ambiguity, referring to the unknowable experience of the other. With this in mind, however, the visual arts can embrace and work with its uncertain communicative power to create new spaces for creativity through a shared distancing and divergence from established social models.

At stake in this study is the role of visual cultures in sustaining critical engagement with the networks and hierarchies of power that generate a synonymy between 'globalisation' and 'global capitalism'. As such, I explore how creative practices can recompose the image of the world, examining the idea of 'the political' to create social ties and networks that sustain the possibility and development of paradigm changes.

World-forming

To address the central question – how can the micro-political interventions of artists and art collectives recompose the image of the world, and why is this significant? – my entry point is through Nancy's writings on 'world-forming'. Reading English translations of Nancy's work, I have been conscious of the transformations and slippages of meaning that take place through translation, particularly with words such as 'mondialisation', which translates into English as 'globalisation', but carries with it an emphasis on 'world-forming', rather than 'globalising' (creating a whole). However, increased awareness of the mutability of these concepts, and of how language generates images and frames concepts of 'the globe', has enabled me to defamiliarise myself with the expression 'globalisation', and its common usage throughout cultural discourses.

What is 'globalisation'? Often, 'globalisation' refers to production, manufacturing and finance, the freeing of trade and economic integration. To briefly summarise a number of different contemporary approaches to globalisation, we might begin by recalling Deleuze and Guattari's writings on 'deterritorialisation', particularly in their 1972 book *Anti-Oedipus*, which draws attention to the significance of *cultural* globalisation as a parallel to political and economic globalisation. By focusing on the deterritorialised exchange of cultural values, Deleuze and Guattari activate discourses on capitalist commodification and the mapping of cultural differences. This raises questions concerning how we might avoid or retreat from commodification.

Some contemporary thinkers, such as anthropologist Arjun Appadurai, have focused on the social imaginary and its political significance in the process of globalisation. Appadurai observes that 'artists are increasingly willing to place high stakes on their sense of the boundaries between their art and the politics of public opinion' and that people progressively 'see their lives through the prisms of the possible lives offered by mass media in all their forms' (1996: 53, 54). For Appadurai, the new social imaginary creates mass cultural aspirations and distances individuals from local cultural identities. The collective social imaginary visualises social possibilities (and impossibilities), meaning that visual cultures increasingly have a social role within the globalising process. However, this also demands that we address the informal and contagious way in which local cultural practices can interrupt and influence this wider cultural imaginary.

In their influential text *Empire*, published in 2000, Hardt and Negri envisage globalisation as an 'empire' that encompasses modern existence – a 'new global form of sovereignty' that hails the decline of the nation-state. Developing Foucault's writings on 'biopower' and examining the power of capitalism, Negri and Hardt form a concept of globalisation that both reflects and generates a sense of cultural, political and economic imbrication. At the outset of the book, they state:

> Our political task, we will argue, is not simply to resist these processes [of globalisation] but to reorganise them and redirect them towards new ends. The creative forces of the multitude that sustain Empire are also capable of autonomously constructing counter-Empire, an alternative political organisation of global flows and exchanges.
>
> (Hardt and Negri 2001: XV)

What might counter-Empire look like, and what role might contemporary art play in the 'reorganisation' of processes of 'globalisation'?

These three different approaches to globalisation illuminate a series of significant questions: How can we avoid being 'captured' by processes of capitalist commodification? What role does creative reflection play in how we conceptualise and imagine the world? And how might a renewed reflection on ontology interrupt and change the way we compose images of the world, perhaps even 'redirecting' processes of globalisation?

Nancy's approach to globalisation offers yet another avenue, but one that can provide a lens through which to confront these questions, further magnifying the significance of contemporary art and cultural practices. He underlines the significance of the *process* of 'mondialisation' or 'worlding' – how we 'form' the world. 'Mondialisation', or 'world-forming', is synonymous with 'globalisation' because these creative actions serve to characterise the 'globe'. The following chapters focus on the (often infinitesimal) creative gestures of contemporary artists and look at how they might redirect and alter wider assumptions that continue to reinforce capitalist images of globalisation. I am interested in the potentially creative forces within globalisation – art practices that offer 'alternative political organisation of global flows and exchanges'. As such, Nancy's concept of world-forming and its emphasis on *how* we 'world' leads into the subject of how creative practices can facilitate critical engagement with the cultural, economic and political apparatuses that constitute globalisation as we know it. Nancy's conceptualisation of both globalisation and world-forming is developed from his ontological theory of 'being singular plural' and this is an important touchstone throughout this book.

To outline the difference between 'globalisation' and 'world-forming', Nancy explains that globality is 'totality as a whole' and therefore nihilistic, because by understanding something as 'a whole' it becomes finite; it is towards-death (CoW 2007c: 27). But for Nancy, another process, that of 'world-forming' happens simultaneously. For Nancy, 'world-forming' is 'absolute immanence' (Raffoul and Pettigrew: CoW 2007c: 5). There is nothing beyond it, because it is the world as praxis, rather than object.

Put simply, Nancy says that world-forming is an ontological process; it is the 'being with' of the world, the exposition of the world to 'being singular plural'. To explain this in a 'singular' ontological way, when I say 'I am', I am positing myself as a finite being, but in acknowledging myself, my consciousness of self is beyond the limits of the 'I' that has been articulated. In this way, a person is always 'with' himself or herself, they are self-aware and therefore each singularity is necessarily plural. 'Being singular plural' is for Nancy the condition of 'being'.

Similarly, 'world-forming' is the infinite process of producing and creating the finite 'things' that together constitute the world. Nancy says that this 'creation' is 'a creation immanent to itself, a creation of itself and for itself' (CoW 2007c: 12). As such, world-forming is absolutely immanent: it both constitutes and exposes the finitude of the world, of being, but it does so infinitely. For Nancy, this awareness of infinity opens out into a kind of abyss, where we realise that there is an absence of a beginning, end and ground. World-forming can either reinforce what already is and unconsciously unfold in accordance with dominant paradigms, or it can be embodied consciously, emphasising creative potential and the possibility of the new. I argue that current systems of capitalist exchange, with their emphasis on forming commensurable, exchangeable things, disregard the 'sense' of the world, but that the conscious embodiment of world-forming emphasises sense and 'incommensurability'.

This study offers a series of reflections on how art practices embody an approach to political discourses based on a sense of how the world forms. By understanding creative interventions[7] as immanent 'world-forming' gestures, I explore how art collectives might facilitate consciousness of social agency that brings with it an increased sense of accountability, and consider how this generates ethical engagement with the practice of recomposing the image of the world. Consequently, rather than referring to 'globalisation', I concentrate on creative practices within these apparatuses, so as to distance the reader from these familiar terms and the assumptions they may carry. Instead, I refer to 'world-forming'.

The Image

What is an 'image'? The word 'image' is rooted in the Latin *imaginem* which indicates a 'likeness' or 'picture', but also carries the meaning 'phantom, ghost, apparition', or metaphorically, an 'idea' or 'appearance'. This sense of separation between the 'appearance' of an identity and an identity itself, is apparent in Nancy's interpretation of the image as 'the distinct' or 'the sacred', as outlined in his essay 'The Image–The Distinct'.[8] By understanding the image as 'the distinct', the viewer recognises that a withdrawal or separation takes place in the creation of an image, rendering it untouchable, but able to evoke a sacred 'force' (GoI 2005: 1–3). Nancy says that the image is 'distinct from all representation', that 'it is an imprint of the intimacy of its passion (of its motion, its agitation, its tension, its passivity)' (GoI 2005: 2, 7). In a key passage in *The Ground of the Image*, Nancy explains the significance of the image in our perception of the 'the world'.

> The image suspends the course of the world and of meaning – of meaning as a course or current of sense (meaning in discourse, meaning that is current and valid): but it affirms all the more a *sense* (therefore an 'insensible') that is *selfsame* with what it gives to be sensed (that is, itself). In the image, which, however, is without an 'inside', there is a sense that is nonsignifying but not insignificant, in a sense that is as certain as its force (its form).
>
> (GoI 2005: 10, 11)

This book explores how seeking to recompose the image of the world is to look at how an image (separate from an 'identity') of the world can become a 'force'/'form' that can 'suspend the course of the world and of meaning'. In other words, I am interested in how recomposing the image of the world can interrupt current, 'validated' capitalist ideologies and affirm sense, consciousness and perception.

Cultural practices, in particular contemporary art interventions, are key to recomposing the image of the world. Nancy writes of how each image is 'a finite cutting out, by the mark of distinction' and that the 'superabundance of images in the multiplicity and in the history of the arts corresponds to this inexhaustible distinction' leading to the infinite opening of, and loss of, 'the *jouissance* of meaning' (GoI 2005: 12, 13). Whilst the significance of the word 'jouissance' shifts depending on its context within Nancy's writing, here, the 'jouissance' of meaning might be understood as the excess of meaning – a temporal enjoyment of meaning that affirms sense as opposed to function. This book looks at how recomposing the image of the world to create a superabundance of images might sustain the infinite 'opening' of the jouissance of meaning, and what this might signify in terms of 'the political'.

An 'Incline' From Ontology to the Political

Writing of the image as 'the distinct', Nancy explains that '[t]he distinct is at a distance, it is the opposite of what is near. What is not near can be set apart in two ways, separated from contact or from identity' (GoI 2005: 2). In this sense, to recompose the image of the world is to create a separation, to withdraw from an apparent identity of the globe and to generate, and be part of 'a co-incidence of an event and an eternity' (GoI 2005: 10). To recompose an image is to withdraw from a fixed identity through creative and critical awareness of the way in which we have conceptualised this identity. I imagine this critical distance as an 'incline' or a slope.

The idea of the image is understood in the context of 'world-forming'. Nancy's concept of the world and of 'world-forming' has developed from his philosophical analysis of 'being'. Stemming from a reinterpretation of the Heideggrarian ontology of 'Dasein', Nancy articulates an ontology of 'being singular plural' or 'being with'. This concept, which is considered in Chapter 2, informs the way in which I approach themes of communication and 'the political' and characterises my relationship to the practices addressed in the following chapters. Nancy calls the development of theory from ontology to the political a 'slope' or 'inclination', and he acknowledges that development of this inclination requires greater analysis. In a colloquium conversation in 2002, quoted by Marie-Eve Morin, Nancy stated that he had not analysed this 'incline' enough (Morin 2012: 113). He recognises that 'being-with' does not immediately constitute a politics but 'allows us to determine the sphere of the political' (Morin 2012: 113).

Two years before (in 2000), Nancy had again reflected on his work with a similar critical analysis. In the French journal *Vacarme*, speaking of his writings relating to *La Comparution*, written with Jean-Christophe Bailly, he stated: 'in writing on "community", on "compearance", then on "being-with", I certainly think I was right to discern the importance of the motif of "the common" and the necessity to work on it anew – but I was wrong when I thought this under the banner of the. . . "political to come"' (2007b). In *Vacarme*, Nancy emphasises that his writings on globalisation, on commonality and on the ontology of 'being with' are political insofar as they *question* the political, rather than proposing a new political essence.

He later continues, in the same article:

> For me, then, the political is from now on submitted to a questioning that must first and foremost bear on the relation and distinction between 'politics' and 'being-in-common'. If you like: the ontology of the common is not immediately political. The most seriously political gesture I can make is to work on this question – no easy task – even if this in no way prevents me from being politically active, in the restricted sense, whenever is necessary.
>
> (2007b)

Nancy's ontology of being singular plural (the ontology of the common) is not instantly 'political' – it does not affirm a particular politics or a positive discourse for specific changes. Rather, it questions and deconstructs perceptions of the political. This critical engagement necessarily concerns the gradual formation and reformation of the political: the processes by which we become aware of, and respond to, the ontology of being singular plural. Consequently, the idea that critical engagement can unfold collectively and create new forms of engagement points to the significance of maintaining creative critique.

An incline can be an ascent or a descent. It indicates a disposition towards something or someone. To visualise the development from ontology to the political as an incline helps us recognise that it involves an inclination or attitude. It situates theory on a gradient of a continuing pathway, where it has a disposition and a context, but agency to move within this context. To trace the incline from ontology to the political is not to aim for a specific destination, but rather to withdraw from a fixed image or an identity and to initiate a distancing. This distancing constitutes and maintains 'the distinct'. The following chapters explore how distancing takes place through the process of recomposing the image of world – a process that requires an inclination away from reinforced perceptions of the world. To acknowledge how the creation of an image 'suspends the course of the world and of meaning' (GoI 2005: 10, 11) is to see how recomposing the image of the world can interrupt meaning and facilitate a 'jouissance' or excess of meaning.

Throughout the book, I approach the idea of political engagement as praxis, rather than as a means to an end. The concept of the political, addressed in greater depth in Chapter 5, ultimately correlates with the idea of ethics. It suggests that political engagement is ultimately critical engagement; the book ultimately advocates an ethical approach that demands 'strength beyond certainty' (Nancy: RtP 1997: 158) – strength that is required to sustain the political as a question, and therefore initiate paradigm changes. Here, 'ethics' no longer refers to universal morals, but rather to the way in which we generate and question the forms of knowledge that characterise morality.

In his 2015 book *After Fukushima: The Equivalence of Catastrophes*, Nancy speaks of the shifts in scale brought about by technologies that are capable of destruction beyond human conception. Changes in the scale of political and social issues are often directly caused by breakdowns of these technologies. Nancy believes that nuclear warheads, for example, introduce a 'balance of terror' in which national security becomes symbolised by the level of threat that each nation wields. For Nancy, this 'balance of terror' breaks down the links between the strong and the less strong in society, and in doing so dissolves the relational structures that characterise and facilitate political engagement (Nancy 2015: 21, 22). In such a political environment, where the *macro*-political paradigms of global capitalism tip the scales of social issues away from the possibility of individual agency, I want to look at how we might reverse this process. By focusing on the micro-political interventions of artists and arts groups, I suggest that it is crucial to sustain and respond to cultural practices during crises. I argue that micro-political cultural practices can create spaces of the 'in-common'; shared cultural spaces in which we can acknowledge increases in the scale of a given issue, but allow for embodied exploration of human agency within these expanding frameworks of consciousness.

Recomposing the Image of the World

The first chapter of the book draws from a number of contemporary thinkers[9] who offer diverse viewpoints on art, politics and globalisation, identifying a number of 'openings' within current discourses – beginnings of a shift in thinking. Chapter 2 explains the relevance of Nancy's philosophy, in particular the concepts of spacing, exscribing and co-appearing. These three actions provide the theoretical base for each of the subsequent chapters of the book. Chapter 2 investigates how Nancy's approach to ontology diverges from phenomenological interpretations of being. This divergence is key to understanding his thinking of 'being singular plural' and being as a shared separation.

With reference to my participation in the political art group Liberate Tate, Chapter 3 considers how communication influences and forms political logics. It begins to analyse how collectives might interrupt and influence larger political discussions. In *The Ground of the Image*, Nancy states that the image seizes us through a contagion (GoI 2005: 9). The chapter builds on Nancy's idea that communication, including visual language, is 'contagious', but that this can be approached with a particular kind of 'intent'.

Chapter 4 approaches Nancy's concept of 'exscribing' through curatorial practices with an arts collective, Art Action UK. Art Action UK is a London-based group of artists, curators, gallerists and writers that offers an annual residency programme for artists who live and work in East Japan and who are responding to the socio-political consequences of the 2011 nuclear disaster. The chapter considers how discourses develop within formal institutional settings.

Chapter 5 develops this theoretical discussion with reference to my role 'evaluating' an exhibition. In 2016, I worked as a volunteer learning assistant at Arnolfini for nine months, which enabled me to read and interpret these texts in practical, concrete terms. It suggests that cultural institutions are able to open up dynamic spaces of 'co-appearance' and discusses the importance of these spaces.

Having started this study participating in the disobedient interventions of Liberate Tate, I close it through reflection on institutional practices. I approach art-making and participating in art (either as a spectator or an actor), as embodied, dynamic practices that function at the limits of, and beyond,[10] the frameworks of global capitalism and neoliberal ideologies. This book is concerned not with how art can carry out pre-formed political ideas, but with how – through art-making and art-viewing – we might recompose images of the world. In particular it looks at how this process of re*com*posing is a *shared* distancing from preconceptions of the world. I am interested in how we co-appear within this shared distancing – creating spaces of appearance in which individuals call into question their opinions and assumptions, and in which new discourses and ways of being together are sparked.

This consequently addresses a concern that emphasis on the *product* of world-forming hinders us from developing and communicating within these spaces. By maintaining an emphasis on 'world-forming', through a focus on spacing, exscribing and co-appearing, this study draws attention to creative processes, the decisions that distinguish and influence these processes and how these might bring about paradigm changes. Approaching these issues through the ontology of being singular plural opens up questions regarding who or what we consider to be agents – therefore situating artists, artworks, spectators and institutions all as agents of social change.

In the article 'Art Today' in the *Journal of Visual Culture*, Nancy states: 'art is there every time to open the world, to open the world to itself, to its possibility of world, to its possibility thus to open meaning, while the meaning that has already been given is closed' (2010). This study culminates in an analysis of how creative practices might 'recompose' – compose again and differently – images of the world: How art can 'open meaning' and facilitate divergence from dominant forms of exchange that characterise globalisation under the dominance of capitalism.

Notes

1. Throughout this book, the term 'global capitalism' refers to non-regulated free-market systems that, transcending national borders, shape social and political ideologies. The complexity of this term, within the current rise of populism, can be seen in the ways in which 'the local' and 'the global' are often placed in opposition in political discourse. Chapter 1 will further address these concepts.
2. The term 'curatorial' refers to the ongoing process of knowledge production, of which an exhibition (or another mode of display) is just a part.
3. Here the term 'socially-engaged art' refers to art that is specifically recognised, in artistic discourse, for how it facilitated participation in a community. However, as this book will argue, all art is 'socially-engaged' in that it engages us with the question of how we are in the world and how we respond to others.
4. Often cited examples include Jeremy Deller's *The Battle of Orgreave* (which reenacted the police response to the miners' strikes of the 1980s, in collaboration with those who actually experienced these events), Santiago Sierra's *Line Tattooed on 6 Paid People, Havana* which controversially addressed the exploitation of workers, and the works of Thomas Hirschhorn created in collaboration with particular communities of people, such as *Gramsci Monument*, which encouraged interaction between people living in a public-housing tower in New York.
5. It would be impossible to comprehensively list these here, but some familiar references would be Chinese dissident artist Ai Weiwei, Russian performance collective Pussy Riot, Japanese artist Megumi Igarashi (who was convicted of circulating 'obscene' images and fined for making a kayak modeled on her vagina) and Cuban artist-activist Tania Bruguera (who was detained by the Cuban authorities and had her passport taken away from her after proposing to create a performance piece about free speech).
6. Although Meillassoux and Nancy forward new readings of 'post-theology', Nancy conceptualises atheism as necessarily relational to theism and looks at how religious ideology develops from pre-religious, philosophical ideas such as 'faith'. Meillassoux, however, criticises the idea of faith, and thinks that Nancy's 'post-theological' faith exposes a limit to his philosophy.
7. I use the phrase 'creative interventions' to discuss creative practices that some would consider 'art activism'. This is a conscious decision to focus on creative processes as critical interruptions and communicative forces, rather than on how these interruptions fail or succeed in terms of any predetermined political effectiveness.
8. Published in the *Heaven* exhibition catalogue in 1999 and again in *The Ground of the Image* (2005).
9. Jacques Rancière, Nicolas Bourriaud Claire Bishop, Grant Kester, Paolo Virno, Chantal Mouffe and Ernesto Laclau, and Bruno Latour.
10. My argument (in brief) is that art-making and art-viewing engages with that which is 'inappropriable', even just temporarily, and for this reason 'beyond' commodification.

1   Art, Politics and Globalisation

This chapter traces the evolution of discourses around art and politics since Bourriaud's influential book *Relational Aesthetics* (1998). I identify particular theoretical positions and perspectives, not to provide exhaustive categories, but with the purpose of highlighting specific questions, gaps and openings within current discourses. With reference to Bruno Latour's writings on 'politics in the new climatic regime' (2018), this chapter discusses how 'globalisation' is bound up in opposing concepts of 'the local' and 'the global'. It argues that by recognising that we are part of the *process* of worlding, we become aware of infinite ways of belonging to the world and that this can impact our conceptualisation of 'the political'. This chapter thus defines the scope of the book and the angle from which I approach the writings of Jean-Luc Nancy.

Re-evaluating Aesthetic Histories

Responding to the linearity of the art historical paradigms that characterised modernist aesthetic theory, Jacques Rancière creates counter-histories. He is a key reference point for a vast number of political art practices because he creates new perspectives on art history. He endeavours to go beyond 'post-structural' theory by critiquing the ways in which aesthetic theories have developed. By focusing on aesthetic fragments of social histories, he is able to deconstruct these histories and re-interpret accepted historic genealogies.

The Politics of Aesthetics (2004) marks Rancière's decisive turn towards aesthetics and defines the scope of his later writings on art and politics. In his essay 'The Distribution of the Sensible: Politics and Aesthetics', Rancière says that it is the 'system of self-evident facts of sense perception that simultaneously discloses the existence of something in common and the delimitations that define the respective parts and positions within it' (2004: 12). However, he concludes the essay by saying:

The arts *only ever lend* to projects of domination or emancipation what they are able to lend to them, that is to say, quite simply, what they have in common with them: bodily positions and movements, functions of speech, the *parcelling out* of the visible and the invisible. Furthermore the autonomy they can enjoy or the subversion they can claim credit for rest on the same foundation.

(2004: 19: emphasis added)

Here, aesthetics is understood as a series of gestures, vocabulary and communications that are all inextricably linked to politics. However, he says that such gestures 'only ever lend' to projects of emancipation, even though their seeming autonomy depends on the same socio-political foundation. The use of the verb 'lend' is significant. For art to 'lend' insinuates that it can also 'retrieve' such gestures, speeches, visible and invisible 'parcels'; that these 'things' are always separate and divisible from a political project of domination or emancipation. Rancière appears to disregard the way in which these moments of commonality affect and transform both the 'project of emancipation' and the art practice itself. Rather than understanding that art is a form of communication that is part of a wider political environment, he reinforces a subtle separation of 'art' and 'projects of emancipation'.

For Rancière, modernism put 'art' and 'life' on a level footing, and whilst maintaining the singularity of aesthetics, decreased the value of this singularity in relation to 'the forms that life uses to shape itself' (2004: 23). As a result, some theorists believe that many 'socially engaged' art practices merely 'dress up' socio-political agendas.[1] Although this is a crucial issue, it is important to understand how ascribing an artwork to an aesthetic regime immediately designates it as illustrative of a larger political agenda. However, if we approach aesthetic practices with a sense that emergent paradigms are fluid and mutable, it is hard to conclusively ascribe them to a specific agenda. Instead, we might start to see how an artwork can *affect politically*, rather than reinforce a perceived consensus.

At the end of the English edition of *The Politics of Aesthetics*, in an interview with the book's translator Gabriel Rockhill, Rancière speaks of 'novelistic micrologies' and says that although there is a limit to the way in which they can 'establish a mode of individuation that comes to challenge political subjectivisation', there is also 'an entire field of play where their modes of individuation and their means of linking sequences contribute to liberating political possibilities by undoing formatting of reality produced by state-controlled media, by undoing the relations between the visible, the sayable, and the thinkable' (2004: 65). For Rancière, aesthetic regimes are initially literary and pictorial before becoming cinematic and photographic, and visual codes are a primary and defining stage within an aesthetic regime (2004: 33).[2] Perhaps the first step in this process is to unmoor aesthetic and political discourses from a perceived 'regime' by looking more closely at its linguistic roots, which in turn destabilise the foundation of the aesthetic regime. Rancière's later book, *Aisthesis: Scenes from the Aesthetic Regime of Art* (2013) begins to do this more pointedly. It mines into the idea of an aesthetic regime and draws upon micro-political details that serve to fragment established aesthetic discourses. He creates multiple counter-histories within modern aesthetic history.

In *Aisthesis*, Rancière explores and defines thought patterns that categorise and interpret artistic spaces. The book consists of 14 'scenes', each of which addresses the 'aesthetic regime of art'. One of his key arguments in the collection is that 'art exists as a separate world since everything whatsoever can belong to it' (2013: X). He states that '[a]rt is given to us through these transformations of the sensible fabric, at the cost of constantly merging its own reasons with those belonging to other spheres of existence' (2013: XI). From the book's prelude, existence is catalogued as having separate 'spheres' and art is situated outside of these, 'given to us' as a specific and assimilable product.

Rancière says that readers of *Aisthesis* 'will be able to construct the history of a regime of art like that of a large fragmented body, and of a multiplicity of unknown bodies born from this very fragmentation' (2013: XIV). By splitting aesthetic histories into such fragments and forms, he initially appears to create an immobile history. His depictions of parts of this 'fragmented body' are separate and detached from the present. However, this process of 'fragmenting', of breaking down histories and re-evaluating and re-framing them, enables 'multiple bodies' to be born and counter-histories to emerge.

Nevertheless, Grant Kester, in *The One and the Many* (2011), critiques the way that Rancière focuses on this process of fragmentation and creation of spaces *between*. Referring to the consensus-based 'third way' of the 1968 protests, which he locates as the root of Rancière's logic, Kester states that he remains 'oddly dependent on an oppositional system of meaning' in which there are only 'active' roles and 'passive' roles that play instrumental parts in 'revealing' a core idea (2011: 102–105). Although Rancière tries to invalidate the opposition between the two roles, he relies on the idea that aesthetics embodies an enigmatic position *between* action and passivity, and believes that aesthetics has a 'civilising' mission that, once achieved, can bring about social and political change (2011: 42, 104). This means that political change, subject to the reformative power of aesthetics, is constantly deferred.

Rancière's method of critique – 'fragmenting' rather than 're-forming' – paradoxically strengthens the historical presence of such a 'regime' within continuing social discourses. Through fragmentation, we are constantly reminded of 'the whole', which rather than disappearing or diminishing, becomes an overarching conceptual presence. Focusing retrospectively on a 'regime', even critically, perhaps hinders or limits interaction with an emergent aesthetic practice. Nonetheless, Rancière's texts provide the initial stage in the development of new political discourses.

In his review of *Aisthesis* in the journal *Parrhesia*, Jean-Philippe Deranty (2013: 140) describes Rancière's 'strategy' by saying that he reduces 'the distance between conceptual elaboration and the object analysed, to transform the object of analysis into the subject of its own conceptuality, to let the subjects of practice unveil the conceptual knots at the heart of their practices'. Rancière's reinterpretation of aesthetic histories enables us to look beyond established aesthetic values and to recover the mechanisms of the perceptions that define them. Following this initial gesture of elucidation, we can begin to unravel, rethink and re-form aesthetic theory.

Negotiating Oppositional Paradigms

Curator and art critic Nicholas Bourriaud arrived at a similar point of exposition to Rancière. Like Rancière, who describes the 'history of a regime of art as being like that of a large fragmented body', which through its fragmentation opens up spaces for 'a multiplicity of unknown bodies' to be born (Rancière 2013: XIV), Bourriaud recognises the need to liberate communicative interaction from modernity, which he depicts as a single historical trajectory and a single body of thought. However, unlike Rancière, he does not excavate aesthetic history or endeavour to fragment it. Rather, he focuses on negotiating the apparent divide between aesthetics and politics that results from this history and that characterises 'post-industrial' society. He uses the term 'relational aesthetics' (also the title of his 1998 book), which has subsequently become a key term in theoretical nomenclature.

Relational Aesthetics (1998) centres around contemporary art's inter-subjectivity and the increasing prevalence of relational art; art defined as much, if not more, by its form as by its final aesthetic product. Bourriaud's collection of essays addresses a central concern that such practices are 'reproached for denying social conflict and dispute, differences and divergences, and the impossibility of communicating within an alienated social space, in favour of an illusory and elitist modelling of forms of sociability, by being limited to the art world' (1998: 82). For Bourriaud, relational practices are predicated on oppositional paradigms: activity/passivity, imaginary/real, creative/schematic. He tries to negotiate the divide *between* these opposites. The importance of the 'gesture' is central to his analysis. In his essay 'Art of the 1990s', he references a wide range of contemporary artworks and says that through 'services rendered, the artists fill in the cracks in the social bond. . . . So through little gestures art is like an angelic programme, *a set of tasks carried out beside or beneath the real economic system, so as to patiently re-stitch the relational fabric*' (1998: 36: emphasis added). Bourriaud again relies on a perceived separation between 'real economic systems' and art systems. By endeavouring to negotiate the divide between aesthetics and 'social bonds' without interrogating the foundations of this divide, he tends to oversimplify artistic practices and characterise them as 'divine' gestures, separate from reality, that serve to *repair* existing social bonds, rather than create new ways of experiencing commonality.

But he does recognise the need to create new 'ways of being together'. In his essay 'Joint Presence and Availability: The Theoretical Legacy of Felix Gonzalez-Torres', he makes the following statement:

> Reintroducing the idea of plurality, for contemporary culture hailing from modernity, means inventing ways of being together, forms of interaction that go beyond the inevitability of the families, ghettos of technological user-friendliness, and collective institutions on offer. . . . In *our post-industrial societies* the most pressing thing is no longer the emancipation of individuals but the freeing-up of interhuman communications, the dimensional emancipation of existence.
>
> (1998: 60: emphasis added)

Bourriaud here prioritises creativity, 'inventing ways of being together' and the 'freeing up' of communication. However, he reinforces a social divide by asserting that social responsibility, and subsequently power, is the duty of 'post-industrial societies'. By declaring 'being together' as dependent on the invention of post-industrial societies, this statement contradicts the emancipatory potential that he is trying to access because it insinuates that free communication is *not* a pressing concern within industrial societies.

Bourriaud's emphasis on embodied communication, on gestures, is a primary concern and although form and aesthetics are important, they are secondary. He recognises that 'form produces and shapes sense, steers it and passes it on into everyday life' (1998: 83). He is concerned with the process of reimagining and reproducing, a process that prevents such projects from becoming familiar, assimilable and dismissible. When Bourriaud states that 'we must thus learn to "seize, enhance and reinvent" subjectivity, for otherwise we shall see it transformed into a rigid collective apparatus at the exclusive service of the powers to be' (1998: 89), he begins to uncover the idea that what is at stake is the *way* in which this transformation unfolds and *how* inclusive such communications are. However, he seems to do this at the expense of material production. He goes so far as to suggest that in contemporary art 'the production of gestures *wins out* over the production of material things' (1998: 103: emphasis added). The measuring of one against the other, of form over aesthetics, unfortunately seems to create a distraction from some of the more progressive nuances in Bourriaud's writing.

The tendency to quantify and compare aesthetics and form is characteristic of much contemporary theory and practice. For many theorists and artists, either material aesthetics define the value of the gesture or the gesture determines the value of the material product. Recent publications, notably Clare Bishop's *Artificial Hells* (2013), focus on the degeneration of aesthetics through the over-emphasis on form. *Artificial Hells* addresses the idea of 'relational aesthetics'. Bishop quotes Bourriaud in his 2002 book *Postproduction: Culture as Screenplay: How Art Reprograms the World*, where he states that 'it is the socius . . . that is the true exhibition site for artists of the current generation' (2012: 207, quoting Bourriaud in *Postproduction* 2002: 65). She understands the socius in this context, 'less in terms of society's users and inhabitants, than as the distributive channels through which information and products flow' (2012: 207). Bishop states that this 'open-endedness stood against the closed meanings of critical art in the '60s and '70s' (2012: 208). This emphasis on the 'flow of information' as an open-ended phenomenon, one that works against the prescription of means and ends, offers a significant shift within aesthetic discourses. Bishop feels that shifts in artistic terminology, for example art as 'project' or a gallery as 'project space', indicate a 'renewed social awareness' which has not been fully theorised (2012: 215).

In her conclusion, Bishop summarises the book's core issue, saying that:

> [the] social discourse accuses the artistic discourse of amorality and inefficiency, because it is insufficient merely to reveal, reduplicate or reflect upon the world; what matters is social change. The artistic discourse accuses the social discourse of remaining stubbornly attached to existing categories, and focusing on micro-political gestures at the expense of sensuous immediacy, as a potential locus of disalienation.
>
> (2012: 276)

This definition of the problematic is perhaps simplistic, referring to both 'artistic discourse' and 'social discourse' as if they were each separate and unified stances.

Bishop references Rancière, saying that for him 'the aesthetic regime is constitutively contradictory, shuttling between autonomy and heteronomy' and that 'there needs to be a mediating object that stands between the idea of the artist and the feeling and interpretation of the spectator' (2012: 278). But does the presence of a mediating object allow for development of theory *beyond* established oppositional paradigms? Might this not continue to facilitate a kind of repetitious ricochet between oppositional paradigms without opening up opportunities for new paradigms to develop?

After calling for a mediating object, Bishop reiterates her belief that it is important to *sustain* tension between social and aesthetic discourses, largely due to what she calls 'the new proximity between spectacle and participation' (2012: 277). She feels that social media has led to a merging of the spectacle with participation, which in turn has generated an 'endless stream of egos levelled to banality' (2012: 277). Grant Kester disputes Bishop, saying that her writings in *Artforum* readily categorise and assume boundaries between 'aesthetic' projects and 'activist' works, defining the former as 'provocative', 'uncomfortable' and 'multi-layered' and the latter as 'predictable', 'benevolent' and 'ineffectual' (2012: 31). Kester believes that by classifying or simplifying these art practices, Bishop fails to acknowledge the importance of 'situationally responsive' work (2011: 32) and instead continues to 'reproduce the epochal consciousness that is typical of the modernist project' in which the positive potential of an artwork is summoned by a lack or loss within a specific historical moment (2011: 30). Kester also includes Bourriaud in his critique, writing that Bourriaud's 'caricature' of socially engaged art practice 'collapses all activist art into the condition of 1930s socialist realism' (2011: 31), and therefore simplifies socially engaged art practices and fails to address the diversity and complexity of such practices.[3] He asserts that, for Bishop and Bourriaud, 'progressive' art, for the most part, has to be provocative and disruptive. It must always act *upon* a given moment in history, a gesture that accentuates the aesthetic and political 'divide'.

Collaborative and Communicative Practice

Kester uses the term 'dialogical art' rather than 'relational art', which sets him apart from the 'post-structural' theorists he critiques. The term 'dialogical art' indicates yet another shift in aesthetic theory. It signifies a conceptualisation of art not as a separate or oppositional force, but as a dynamic and engaged form of communication. Such communication is never 'complete', nor does it negate or 'act on' histories. Rather, it continues to inform these histories and to be informed by them. 'Dialogical art' approaches communicative gestures as multi-layered and 'incalculable' signs that have meaning and power but are not reducible to a single 'truth'.

This approach requires a constant letting go of 'knowledge'. Kester's fundamental argument can be summed up in his concluding words: 'the creation of new knowledge regarding political and social transformations and the specific role that art can play in facilitating this transformation, requires the process of both *learning and un-learning via practice*' (2011: 226: emphasis added). As we have seen, Kester feels that other theorists do not sufficiently recognise the complex registers and site-specific nuances of socially engaged art practices. He feels that they are too closely bound to what he defines as post-structural ideologies[4] that subsume the radical potential of such practices because they approach them with assumptions based on specific art historical canons and ultimately situate them as nothing more than illustrations of art theory (2011: 54–56).

For this reason, Kester focuses on what he calls (referring to artistic practices in Myanmar) 'the complex choreography of communicative interaction: the ways in which the cognitive and the haptic, action and movement, pose and gesture' that produce (and defer) meaning (2011: 149). It is this focus on the gestures that constitute a micro-political intervention that, for me, sparks a new way of approaching such practices as an engaged theorist. Kester draws upon the significance of the deferral of meaning as well as its production and looks at each case study as a small microcosm in itself, and how each practice generates political questions within a global context, rather than presenting specific practices as emblems of pre-formed academic discourses.

Kester thinks that post-structural philosophers such as Derrida, Foucault and Deleuze have supervised the process of 'privileging dissensus over consensus, rupture and immediacy over continuity and duration' and have built up 'extreme scepticism about organised political action' (2011: 54). He believes that post-structuralism is all about artists and writers enabling the 'ethical normalisation of desire and somatic or sensual experience' (2011: 54) and that this leads to the distancing of the artist and the viewer. Here the artist has a 'custodial role' and the viewer is always 'acted upon' (2011: 54). Whilst he makes a valid and important point about certain trends and their effect within the art world, he tends to generalise and to categorise many different thinkers as 'post-structuralist', even hinting at a kind of ideological co-option when he writes of 'thinkers who stormed the Sorbonne' and states that they constitute 'a kind of globalised theoretical *lingua franca* in the arts and humanities' (2011: 54).[5] Ironically, in describing the limitations of these writings through limited references to their works, Kester readily commits their writing to a particular time and shuts down the potentiality of the nuances and complexities of these writings.

Kester's shift from relational theory, which tended to reinforce difference, to dialogical theory, which deconstructs oppositional paradigms, begins to create a kind of communicative synthesis that allows for a more nuanced understanding of contemporary art practices. But to develop this further it is necessary to look in much greater detail at the concept of communication.

Paulo Virno's exploration of semantics in his 2008 book *Multitude: Between Innovation and Negation* undertakes a finely detailed analysis of communication and its political significance, and is a point of reference in many articles and texts on art activism.[6] For Virno, our modes of communication are evidence of bioanthropological traits that distinguish people from animals.[7] Virno develops the idea of language and ritual as 'institutions'. He says that language 'concerns the single human animal only in as much as this animal is part of a "mass of speakers". Just like freedom or power, it exists only in the relation between the members of a community' (2008: 46). For Virno, language concerns 'the unknown' as well as 'the habitual' (2008: 49); it has no limits and yet it can close in on itself. He talks about the 'excess of semanticity', which 'is equivalent to a state of shapeless potentiality' and the 'defect of semanticity', which can lead to the over-definition and reduction of discourses into stereotypes: 'the world dries up and is simplified to the point of resembling a papier-mâché backdrop' (2008: 52). It is this tension that communication (and therefore visual language) negotiates. There is a risk that discourses can be articulated so thoroughly that they serve to negate their own potential. This question of communicability echoes Kester's solicitation to 'unlearn' as well as to learn.

Regarding communication, as the sharing of meaning through language, Virno develops a concept of the world stemming from the excesses and defects of semanticity. He understands the 'world' as 'a vital context that always remains partially undetermined and unpredictable' and aligns himself with Helmuth Plessner (whom Carl Schmitt writes about in depth), who understands humans as animals 'open to the world' (2008: 17). To paraphrase briefly, humans are animals that are determined by behavioural and physical characteristics, but they are also able to maintain a distance or separation from the state in which they exist. For this reason, humans are able to be 'open to the world'; to value indeterminacy.

One of Virno's central questions is: 'In what way can excessive drive and the opening to the world serve as a political antidote to the poison that they themselves secrete?' (2008: 24). Simply put, how can man's openness to the world perpetuate a freedom that perpetuates *further* freedom, rather than a recklessness that ultimately restricts openness to the world (for example violence that increases danger at the 'opening to the world')? Virno begins to trace a pathway between subjectivity, semantics and political engagement, and he draws out ethical and moral questions about how to negotiate the development from one to the other, often drawing on theological imagery. Whilst he refers to biblical metaphors, he traces their meaning back to basic philosophical questions that can be applied within a much wider theoretical framework. This highlights the Western bias of his writing but simultaneously begins to uncover mechanisms within Western thought.

Conceptualising 'the World'; Political Art Practices and Globalisation

Virno writes in detail about the biblical and political philosophy of 'katechon'. In a biblical context, the katechon is a force that limits evil by encompassing it and holding it within itself, but at the same time it provides the possibility of redemption. Virno says that katechon 'brings into check the excess and defect of semanticity'. It 'delays the end of the world. But the opening to the world, the stigma of the linguistic animal, consists precisely in this constantly renewed deferral' (2008: 60). At the heart of the concept of the katechon we find interdependent oppositional forces. This antagonistic tension is necessary for the continual formation of, rather than consolidation of, 'the world', a tension that resists both 'shapeless potentiality' and reductive stereotyping.

Although very different in scope from Virno's theories, the writings of political theorists Chantal Mouffe and Ernesto Laclau focus on the interdependence of art practitioners, activists and institutions and the significance of intercommunicative tensions that maintain and encompass difference. Mouffe's articulation of 'agonistics' advocates the need for dissensus to sustain openness to the world, and perhaps to sustain what Virno describes as 'constantly renewed deferral'.

In the preface to the 2014 edition of the (1985) book *Hegemony and Socialist Strategy: Toward a Radical Democratic Politics*, Laclau and Mouffe argue: 'Presented as driven exclusively by the information revolution, the forces of globalisation are detached from their political dimensions and appear as a fate to which we all have to submit' (2014: XVI). They reassert the need for democratic inter-communication within the development of 'globalisation'. Globalisation is often understood as a kind of independent capitalist force that eclipses micro-political discourses. For Mouffe and Laclau, this global capitalist force is just one way in which the world functions: there are alternatives. *Hegemony and Socialist Strategy* calls for a re-interpretation of global political dynamics. It highlights the need for antagonisms and political tensions that sustain a more open and democratic development of global politics.

For Mouffe and Laclau, the crucial problem with liberal democracy is that it 'envisages democracy as simple competition among interests taking place in a neutral terrain – even if the accent is put on the "dialogic dimension"' (2014: XVI). This diminishes the possibility of establishing a new hegemony, and marginalises anti-capitalist elements that had previously been more present in both right- and left-wing ideologies. In a much later essay, 'Institutions as Sites of Antagonistic Intervention', Mouffe advocates a 'radical critique fostering a strategy of "engagement with institutions"' that enables us to envisage the conditions of a 'radical democratic' (2014: 68). Acknowledging, and working with, discordant dynamics in this engaged dialogue actively works against the binary categorisation applied to so many practices, a categorisation that often reduces both the potentiality of a political art gesture and the social value of an institution.

As discussed earlier, theorists such as Grant Kester criticise the disruptive nature of dissensus and consider it to have a traumatic impact. Mouffe, on the other hand, suggests that if we are prepared for discord and accept it as a necessary political tension, rather than striving to create a perfectly harmonious, utopian society, we will be more able to develop new ways of addressing socio-political concerns, without experiencing dissensus as a traumatic 'shock'.

'The Local' and 'the Global'

The word 'globalisation' often refers to the idea of a single cultural and/or economic narrative imposed throughout the world. In the introduction, I briefly referenced texts that acknowledged how this imposition can encompass modern existence, affecting the social imaginary and accelerating commodification in all spheres of our lives. As outlined, theorists are calling for ideological and behavioural shifts to counter this single narrative. A key text to help us reorient discourses surrounding globalisation is sociologist Bruno Latour's 2018 book *Down to Earth: Politics in the New Climatic Regime*.

Latour deconstructs the concepts of 'the global' and 'the local' – two poles that have characterised our perceptions of the world and our position 'within' it. Progress is often seen as a trajectory from the local to the global. He explains that, although within each of these concepts there is a 'plus' and 'minus' version, tracing (in either direction) the trajectory between the 'the global' and 'the local' merely sustains illusions of destinations that can never be reached. He explains that the earth cannot accommodate the 'globe' of globalisation, and at the same time, it is too expansive to remain within the limits of a 'locality'.

Instead of focusing on 'the local' and 'the global', Latour foregrounds the concept of the 'Terrestrial' and asks us to understand that a 'new site of politics' is emerging (2018: 40). He explains: 'the Terrestrial is not yet an *institution*, but it is an actor whose role is clearly different from the political role attributed to "nature" by the Moderns' (2018: 89). For centuries, following the promise of 'progress', we have viewed nature as something separate, something to gain mastery over. Latour proposes that we understand nature as a *process* that we are a part of (2018: 75). It is significant here that he describes the Terrestrial (the new political actor) as 'not yet an institution' – as explained in the introduction, Nancy's philosophy is 'pre-institutional'. In this book, I am interested in practices and collectives that are 'not yet institutions', but also the 'not yet' that is part of existing cultural institutions.

Acknowledging that we are part of the *process* of nature, a process of worlding, allows us to challenge the concepts of 'the local' and 'the global'. Understanding that we are part of the process of nature demands that we understand that we are agents amongst others, and that we constitute the world (rather than live 'in' the world or 'on' earth). Consequently, we become aware of the lack of mastery we have, and of the futility of either continuing to move towards the 'infinite horizon' of the Global, or turning back towards the Local and its promise of stability and sense of 'assured identity' (Latour 2018: 42). Instead of moving between these two poles, Latour calls for 'everything to be mapped out anew' (2018: 33) through the political agent of the Terrestrial. He writes: 'In the end, what counts is not knowing whether you are for or against globalization, for or against the local; all that counts is understanding whether you are managing to register, to maintain, to cherish a maximum number of alternative ways of belonging to the world' (2018: 15, 16). This reinforces the central argument of this book – that we must continue to recompose the image of the world, again and again, as much as we can, and to cherish appreciation of the infinite ways of belonging to the world.

This chapter has aimed to trace theoretical discourses around art, politics and globalisation to show how contemporary thought is gradually moving away from the idea of a single narrative (albeit fragmented) that has been supplemented, or even 'patched up' (to paraphrase Bourriaud) by artistic practices. It has suggested that art, as creative visual language, is part of the communicative practice that negotiates a tension between over-definition and 'shapeless potentiality' (Virno 2008: 52). As such, it is proposing that art allows us to 'cherish a maximum number of alternative ways of belonging to the world' (Latour 2018: 16), creatively responding to a variety of agents that constitute the world. Here, the differentiation between art and politics is no longer appropriate, because art (and, more broadly, creative visual communication) plays a key role in the development of a new climatic regime. The next question is: Why approach this role through reading the philosophy of Jean-Luc Nancy? The following chapter considers how reading Nancy can further elucidate, and build on, these perspectives.

Notes

1. This is the premise for Claire Bishop's 2013 *Artificial Hells*, which draws largely from Rancière's conceptualisation of aesthetics, and opens with a critique of the cultural policies of the 1997–2010 "New Labour" UK government, which used art as a legislative tool.

2. Brian Holmes, in his essay 'Hieroglyphs of the Future: Jacques Rancière and the Aesthetics of Equality', states that the 'originality of Rancière's work on the aesthetic regime is to clearly show how art can be historically effective and directly political. Art achieves this by means of fictions: arrangements of signs that *inhere* to reality, yet at the same time make it legible to the person moving through it' (2001). This sums up the way in which Rancière articulates and begins to deconstruct aesthetic histories and fictions. However, as Holmes points out, for Rancière these signs 'inhere' to reality, and it is this separation from reality that I would like to flag and call into question.

3. He is critical of the idea that art has an 'instrumentalising relationship to the material, against which art is defined' (2011: 35) and he believes Bishop and Bourriaud advocate this because they look for 'progress' in art and for that reason 'fix' the meaning of an artwork (2011: 35).

4. For example, for Kester, Rancière's thought is bound up in the Deleuzian/Spinozian idea that 'until we overcome our naive faith in our own conscious agency and come to recognize the "hidden" laws that structure and predetermine our ostensibly vocational actions, we will remain in "bondage"' (2011: 182). Kester believes that this leads to a belief in 'set' principles and in turn over-emphasises the value of 'shocks'.

5. Kester's tendency to make such generalisations is especially evident when he later writes about Nancy, who he describes as 'emblematic' of the idea that art must be the 'inverse of labor' (2011: 104). In short, Kester ignores Nancy's thread of logic that questions the approach to art as a site of production. Whilst Nancy understands art as a creative gesture, rather than positing it as the inverse of labour, he understands it as an 'excess' of labour, something that is not merely a tool to carry out a particular function, but something that operates *beyond* a function.

6. For more on this, see Alexei Penzin's interview with Virno in *Meditations Journal* no. 25, titled 'The Soviets of the Multitude: On Collectivity and Collective Work: An Interview with Paolo Virno', 2010.

7. 'Bioanthropology' is a key term and concept in the book. Virno addresses politics and language through an examination of biological and behavioural patterns, how these form the dynamics that sustain particular social relations.

2 Jean-Luc Nancy and Contemporary Art

Nancy has written extensively about art and for exhibitions and projects. This part of his oeuvre includes exhibition texts and essays, and he has influenced conceptual threads in a number of films. Nancy has collaborated on projects with artist Phillip Warnell and his 2000 autobiographical essay *L'intrus* inspired a film of the same name by Claire Denis. Whilst these significant texts clearly place Nancy's philosophy into the context of contemporary cultural practices, they are not main theoretical reference points for this book. Because my focus is on the incline from ontology to the political, I have chosen to centre my analysis on texts that have a broader analysis of philosophy, community and the political. Nevertheless, Nancy's close attention to individual artworks can provide a powerful lens onto key ideas such as spacing and singularity. For this reason, this chapter will explore two of Nancy's key texts on art – *The Ground of the Image* and *The Muses* – texts that consider singularities and praxis within the context of contemporary art and provide insights that help plot the incline from ontology to the political. The chapter will also explain how Nancy's understanding of the subject leads to a 'quasi-ontology' that can help us question, and think beyond, the perceived divide between art and politics, explored in the previous chapter.

Art as Exposition

In *The Ground of the Image*, Nancy states that an image has 'force', that it affirms sense and suspends meaning – a suspension that interrupts our sense of the world and alters how we experience the world around us (GoI 2005: 10, 11). In his writings on art, he frequently turns to well-known images. In *Being Nude: The Skin of Images*, his poetic readings of specific paintings such as Rembrandt's *Bathsheba in the Bath* and Goya's *The Nude Maja* firmly contextualise his philosophy within the field of art theory. Importantly, they recompose images of these famous artworks, asking readers to look at these images again differently. Why is it important to 'recompose' such images? Writing of the distance between the audience and nudes in painting and photography, Nancy states:

> This ambiguous proximity is also an opportunity for thought, if, for thought, it is a matter above all else of remaining stripped bare of all received meaning and figures that have already been traced. The nudes of painters and photographers expose this bareness and suspense on the edge of a sense that is always nascent, always fleeting, on the surface of the skin, and on the surface of the image.
>
> (Nancy 2014b: 4)

Here we read familiar vocabulary, such as 'expose' and 'sense'. 'Sense' is a fundamental concept in Nancy's philosophy – it refers to the *shared exposition* of singularities (human and object). Sense is a receptivity that takes place prior to clear-cut thought. Sense is 'always nascent'. Nancy turns to the image as a 'surface' that provides an 'edge' of incommensurable sense. Here, images expose a bareness, an absence that gives a sense of suspense and possibility. Without this sense, it is impossible to imagine alternative images of the world and possibilities for being.

Later in this collection of essays, Nancy reflects on the role of the image as 'a manner of presence' (2005: 66). He says that '[s]ense requires the image in order to emerge from its meagre material, its inaudibility and its indivisibility. Sense requires sound, line and figure, without which it is as abstract and fugitive as the movement of a needle through the stitches of a piece of lace' (GoI 2005: 67). Here, we see that 'sense' requires an image, but at the same time, the image functions by 'making *absence* a presence' because it 'does not do away with the impalpable nature of absence' and is concerned solely with 'immateriality' (GoI 2005: 67: emphasis added). This complexity in Nancy's approach to the image is spotlighted by John Paul Ricco in his 2014 book *The Decision Between Us: Art and Ethics in the Time of Scenes*, where he points out that the image is the 'scene of a shared exposure to the infinite finitude of existence', and that it stages an intimate 'shared-separation' (2014: 29). This is a crucial observation to bear in mind before approaching the ontological significance of Nancy's writings. As Ricco emphasises, the image is an '*aporetic spacing* – a suspended path and a path of suspension' (2014: 137: emphasis added). For Ricco, Nancy's philosophy is dedicated to an 'unbecoming ontology of exposition and exposure' (2014: 86), explored through the concept of 'spacing'. Departing from this idea of an 'unbecoming' ontology, the next stage of my analysis will be to consider how 'spacing' embodies this philosophy of being. Ricco suggests that, for Nancy, 'existence is its own essence', and as such becomes 'divorced' from the ontological (2014: 75–76). The following chapters will reflect on this idea, and the possibility that Nancy's philosophy of being revolves around a continual process of '*divorcing*' which reaffirms the body as the site of ontology.

How might the intimacy of the shared exposure of bodies, and its subsequent scene or image, relate to the image of the world? In *The Ground of the Image*, Nancy gives the example of a literary image (from Edith Wharton's *Summer*) – the image of a girl standing on the doorstep of a building, framed by a village and surrounding countryside. He says:

> with the 'girl' . . . an entire world 'comes out' and appears, a world that also 'stands on the doorstep', so to speak. . . : a world that we enter while remaining before it, and that thus offers itself fully for what it is, a *world*, which is to say: an indefinite totality of meaning (and not merely an environment).
>
> (2005: 4, 5)

For Nancy, this image has an 'intimate force', not in terms of what it represents, but through the force of the image represent*ing* – the ability of an image to touch consciousness (GoI 2005: 5). This intimate force appears as 'a world' – in writing this image, and in imagining it, we participate in composing an image of this world. If, with Nancy, we understand the 'world' as the 'indefinite totality of meaning' that constitutes our consciousness of others' differing perceptions of the world, this creative gesture (of composing an image of this representation) recomposes the image of the world. Understanding the image as something that has an intimate force, that is a site of absence into which we cannot enter, has bearings on the central idea of recomposing the image of the world. An image appears as that which is absent – it exposes a separation. Consequently, the process of recomposing is facilitated by the way in which being 'spaces' or 'divorces' itself from ontology, from already formed concepts and categories that show a set of existing properties and relations. To recompose the image of the world is to constantly affirm this separation or 'divorcing' of being, and to affirm its potentiality.

In *The Muses*, Nancy addresses the plurality of arts and the plurality of worlds. The book's opening essay – 'Why Are There Several Arts and Not Just One? (Conversation on the Plurality of Worlds)' – considers the way in which art is singular plural. Nancy writes, 'Art isolates or forces there the movement of the *world* as such, the being world of the world, not as does a milieu in which a subject moves, but its exteriority and exposition of a being-in-the-world, exteriority and exposition that are formally grasped, isolated and presented as such' (M 1996: 18). Here, 'being-in-the-world' refers to the 'very springing forth' of being, its 'spacing'. The plurality of artistic expressions amplifies the singularity of art, particularly when these expressions or practices push the boundaries of what we think of as art. Art, as a formal presentation of exteriority, should not be thought of in terms of the subject, but in terms of singularity. Nancy imagines art's singularity as always 'just around the bend', not fully perceptible as 'art' and just beyond our full comprehension (M 1996: 4). The obliqueness of art is what constitutes something as 'art' and characterises 'the problem of art': 'The singular plural/singular is the law and the problem of art', Nancy writes, 'as it is of "sense" or of the sense of the senses, of the sensed sense of their sensuous difference' (M 1996: 13-14). This absent singularity – a singularity that is just around the bend – means that art remains ungraspable even as we can sense it.

When Nancy writes of 'exteriority and exposition of a being-in-the-world' (M 1996: 18), he reminds us that he understands 'being-in-the-world' as synonymous with 'being-*of*-the-world' (M 1996: 19). He is keen to emphasise that we are singular plural and therefore part of the world (and constituting the world); we are not separate subjects *within* the world. What does it mean to 'formally grasp' exposition? Surely a 'formal grasp' serves to affirm a particular signification and to adhere to a convention, and Nancy clearly writes that art 'disengages the world from signification', that it 'dislocates' common sense (M 1996: 22). This dislocation allows us to critically engage with what we might consider to be normal or ordinary, and calls for a new way of being-with. Here, Nancy's use of the word 'formally' evokes a sense of seriousness, a sense of something being done in a 'correct' way. But this correctness does not accord to a predetermined etiquette or ethics; it is a correctness that is 'in its own right'.

Later in the same essay, Nancy writes of the limits of phenomenology when 'the single theme of an "appearing" cannot respond to the clear-cut – and cutting – discreteness of a ground that withdraws and retraces itself in forms' (1996: 32).[1] He goes so far as to say that the 'things of art' are 'themselves phenomenology . . . because they are in advance of the phenomenon itself' (1996: 33). Nancy's descriptions of art as 'formal' and 'discrete' help us understand that art is immanent, that it is a 'patency' (1996: 34) – an openness that cannot be reduced or measured with relation to other 'things'. Through this very patency, art is always in advance of signification and is not answerable to anything other than itself. Art is the presentation of presentation, the presentation of 'spacing'.

Some years later, Nancy briefly returns to this idea of 'discreteness' in relation to spacing in *Being Singular Plural*. In the context of speaking of the 'Other', he says that 'Being is not the Other, but the origin is the punctual and discrete spacing *between us*, as *between us and the rest of the world, as between all beings'* (BSP 2000: 19). Here he uses the adjectives 'punctual' and 'discrete' to describe spacing, words that connote formality. Could spacing be the opposite – 'belated' or 'attached'?

The word 'discrete' implies a separation or distinction. In the context of understanding art as a singularity, one that is 'just around the bend', this discreteness refers to the separating that constitutes being. This separation or distinction constitutes the exteriority and exposition of being. And it is this sense that is 'grasped, isolated and presented' in art.

'Punctual' implies that something happens at a 'proper' time. To consider spacing as happening at an 'improper' time implies an inappropriate gesture, one that is relational to an intended outcome. But spacing cannot 'fail' or be 'improper', because it is necessarily open to possibility. By the same token, it cannot be 'proper' in a relational sense, because it is indeterminable and open to the contingent. However, it is 'punctual' in that it is *proper to itself*; it is 'on time'. Spacing is synonymous with time as an irreversible continuum.

Art practices embody this exposition, both through the creative performance of making an artwork, and through the way in which audiences and participants engage with art. Making a deconstructive political gesture through art, rather than through traditional means of protest, calls for different engagement. It calls for attention to how we are 'of-the-world', how we can embody a patency that makes space for social change.

Nancy's 'Quasi-ontology'

Nancy moves away from traditional phenomenology to develop an understanding of being singular plural rather than individuality. This has significance in terms of how this study approaches ideas of communication and community, and consequently the political.

Nancy's writings challenge and deconstruct the idea of 'the subject'. For Nancy, the concept of the subject often affirms ideas of 'individuality', 'essence' and 'value', and consequently the idea of 'mastery' (WCATS 1991: 4). Critique of 'the subject' provides the starting point for the 1991 collection *Who Comes After the Subject?* – a collection edited by Nancy, Eduardo Cadava and Peter Connor – in which the use of 'who' focuses the reader on that which 'comes indefinitely to itself, never stops coming, arriving: the "subject" that is never the subject of itself' (WCATS 1991: 7). Put differently, Nancy conceives of presence as a dynamic coming-to presence, a 'taking place'. In *Who Comes After the Subject?* Nancy states '[t]he coming into presence is plural' (WCATS 1991: 8). He later (in 2000) published *Being Singular Plural*, but this idea of coming to presence as a *shared* appearing, characterises his approach to ontology, from his early writings (collected in *The Birth to Presence*), right through to *The Disa-vowed Community*.

In *The Inoperative Community*, published the same year as *Who Comes After the Subject?*, Nancy explains that 'the *I* is something other than a subject' and he writes: 'That which is not a subject opens up and opens onto a community whose conception, in turn, exceeds the resources of a meta-physics of the subject' (IC 1991a: 14). As such he writes of 'being singular plural' and consequently of 'singularities' rather than 'subjects'. What are 'singularities' and how do they 'exceed the resources of a metaphysics of the subject'? Nancy challenges the idea of the subject as *that which causes* things, and instead he draws attention to the limits of this metaphysics. 'Singularity' concerns the relationality of being. This relation exposes the non-absoluteness of being. Nancy clearly states: 'singularity never has the nature or the structure of individuality' (IC 1991a: 6). Accordingly, referring to 'singularities' and 'being singular plural' rather than 'subjects' allows us to sustain awareness of the incommensurability of being and reminds us of the relational nature of community.

In his introduction to the *The Inoperative Community*, Christopher Fynsk explains:

> While a singular being may come to its existence as a subject only in this relation (and it is crucial, in a political perspective, to note that Nancy thus starts from the *relation* and not from the solitary subject or individual), this communitary 'ground' or condition of existence is an unsublatable differential relation that 'is' only in and by its multiple singular articulations (though it is always irreducible to these) and thus differs constantly from itself.
>
> (IC 1991: X)

Singularity is unidentifiable – it is characterised by the way in which a sin-gular being is exposed to shared 'otherness' and shared finitude (IC 1991a: 23). This exposure invalidates the perception of a solitary subject, so that the concept of the individual lingers only as 'the residue of the experience of the dissolution of community' (IC 1991a: 3). What is important to Nancy is how being is constituted by shared separation, the condition for com-munication and community. Importantly, singularity does not originate in anything (it does not originate in an individual 'subject') but is a relation that calls to attention the non-absoluteness of a singular being.

What is unique about Nancy's approach to ontology? As we know, ontol-ogy is the field of thought that branches from metaphysics to focus on the nature of being, and how this constitutes reality and its properties – the ontic. For Nancy, writing in *Being Singular Plural*, ontology is, canonically, first philosophy – exploring the nature of being is the primary way of thinking philosophically about reality. However, he says that philosophy needs to 'recommence' and 'to think in principle how we are "us" among us, that is how the consistency of our Being is in being-in-common, and how this consists precisely in the "in" or in the "between" of its spacing' (BSP 2000: 25, 26). He describes his thinking of 'being with' as a 'minimal ontological premise' structured by the 'spacing' of things and people (BSP 2000: 27, 28). Accordingly, Nancy introduces his interpretation of ontology as the 'being with of all that is' that is 'itself bare and impossible to evaluate' (BSP 2000: 4). Here we can see that Nancy's thinking regarding ontology spotlights the *relation* between ontology and the ontic, and this emphasis on relationality means that the concept of 'spacing' cannot be assimilated into a category of ontology. In turn, this demands the 'recommencing' of thinking and prevents the finitude of philosophical thought or the closure of the philosophical 'field' of ontology. Perhaps for this reason, Nancy articulates the need to rethink the 'incline' between ontology and the political. His writings suggest that reflecting on the *relation between* ontology and the ontic can alter the development of theory and its influence. This is a kind of 'quasi-ontology', a term I will use to distinguish Nancy's understanding of ontology as the 'spacing' or 'distancing' that causes things and people to appear. As outlined, I am interested in how Nancy's quasi-ontological stance characterises his interpretation of the image and how recomposing an image generates a conscious spacing from, but relation to, the ontic.

Nancy's quasi-ontology differs from ontological analyses in phenomenology. It demands relinquishing the idea of 'the subject'. In simple terms, phenomenology frames phenomena as subjective – rooted in human consciousness – and affirms the existence of 'subjects' and 'objects'. The word 'phenomenology' (*phainomenon*) indicates the study of appearances. To approach an idea phenomenologically is to look at how events happen to individuals and are experienced by separate subjectivities. This consequently leads to analysis of how individuals act with intent towards objects. Although Nancy writes extensively on 'appearing' – as will be considered in Chapter 5 – he approaches it through his quasi-ontology.

Although ontology is the study of 'what is' (as opposed to phenomenology which is the study of what appears), Nancy asserts that 'what is' is not fixed or absolute, and that it appears as contingent and incommensurable, as a spacing that exposes shared separation. For Nancy, therefore, the idea of appearing characterises his quasi-ontology. In *The Sense of the World*, Nancy clearly articulates this idea: 'the *world* invites us to think no longer on the level of the phenomenon, however it may be understood (as surging forth, appearing, becoming visible, brilliance, occurrence, event), but on the level . . . of the dis-position (spacing, touching, contact, crossing)' (SoW 1997: 176). Philip Armstrong, in his essay 'From Appearance to Exposure', spotlights this passage and goes on to describe the term 'spacing' as 'touching on or *at* the very limits of the phenomenological tradition' (2010: 18). Nancy touches at the limits of the phenomenological tradition because he destabilises the idea of appearing as the appearing of a subject or object, but rather as the appearing of an absenting presence (a shared-separated spacing). For Nancy, being is characterised through a shared spacing, a shared awareness of the incommensurability of the other. In *The Fragmentary Demand*, Ian James comments, 'it is more true to say that, like Derrida's thought, Nancy's philosophy grows out of phenomenology in general and could more properly be characterized as post-phenomenological' (2006: 39). In this way he neither adheres to, nor entirely rejects, phenomenology.

Armstrong references James, who later states that Nancy's 'decisive break from phenomenology . . . occurs, perhaps, at a moment of greatest proximity or closeness to the phenomenological account' (2006: 96). Armstrong comments: 'Nancy's affirmation of exposure in his writings becomes most resonant when dealing with descriptions of phenomenological appearance' (2010: 17). For Nancy, appearing indicates the shared separation of being-with and, as Armstrong reminds us, 'there is no "in itself" that is not already immediately "with"' (2010: 17). So where Nancy's writings touch on phenomenology, they do so in order to complicate and question the idea of appearing as a simply phenomenological matter, concerning subjects and objects, instead asking us to reconsider what 'appearing' really is. Following Nancy, we can begin to understand being and appearing in terms of ontological spacing.

Beyond the Art/Politics Divide

As contemporary discourses move beyond the art/politics divide, there are still vital questions and ideas that demand critical philosophical analysis. The following paragraphs explain how Nancy's philosophical writings address specific gaps in the contemporary art and political theory explored in Chapter 1.

As outlined in Chapter 1, Rancière's writings act as a deconstructive gesture. He fragments aesthetic histories, allowing us to understand how counter-histories can emerge. Nancy's writings travel further down this pathway of rethinking and re-forming aesthetic theory. He approaches semiology in a way that acknowledges concrete aesthetics, but his writings open meaning to new contexts.

This approach is illustrated by Nancy's writing style. In the introduction to her book *Jean Luc Nancy*, Marie-Eve Morin says that although Nancy defines things in a concrete way (x = y), he continues to define and re-establish meaning within a given context, i.e., x = y but then y = z. She says that this creates a 'circular meaning' and that our perception and understanding of Nancy's thoughts, its meaning, should be found in this continual movement of understanding, so that the 'concepts start to *make* sense' (2012: 5). This mode of communication resonates with Nancy's perception of being and consciousness. For Nancy, 'to "happen" is neither to flow (to disappear), nor to grow, nor to be purely present but to be continuously in the movement of arriving or 'acceding'" (2012: 33), so that to 'understand' is never a fully completed process, but is exposed to incomprehension.

Bourriaud's spotlight on 'the gesture' highlights new questions regarding communicative actions, especially when he claims that in contemporary art 'the production of gestures wins out over the production of material things' (1998: 103). Bourriaud references Guattari, for whom 'aesthetics must above all else go hand in hand with societal changes, and inflect them' (1998: 104). Key to Bourriaud's approach to art is that 'imagination seems like a prosthesis affixed to the real so as to produce more intercourse between interlocutors. So the goal of art is to reduce the mechanical share in us. Its aim is to destroy any a priori agreement about what is perceived' (1998: 80). Both Bourriaud and Nancy believe in the powerful agency of the imagination and of 'jouissance'. However, rather than destroying the 'a priori agreements about what is perceived', Nancy acknowledges the grounds that such agreements provide for the imagination. In other words, the real and the imaginary are part of a dynamism that characterises consciousness, or following Bourriaud, they produce 'intercourse between interlocutors'. Nancy focuses on this dynamic relationship, the movement beyond that which is already there, as his starting point.

Virno often writes of the 'linguistic animal' and the 'political animal' as two separate beings, but for Nancy, communication is initiated by, and yet beyond, linguistics, but is nevertheless a pre-requisite for politics. Communication allows for political engagement and the two are inseparable. However, like Nancy, Virno understands the 'world' as a 'vital context that always remains partially undermined and unpredictable' (2008: 17) and his writings on the excess and defect of semanticity introduce an ethical concept of managing semantics in a way that creates a 'political antidote' to the evils secreted in the 'world' (2008: 24). Although Nancy understands 'communication' in a broader sense than semantic exchange, Virno's writings on semantics relate to the principles within the interpretation and production of meaning. Virno therefore offers a critical perspective on Nancy's writings, by looking beyond the creation of meaning and addressing the inevitable tensions within *governance* of meaning.

Kester, in his generalisation of 'post-structural' theory, interprets Nancy's idea of an un-worked community as a reduction of 'all human labour to a simple expression of conative aggression, functioning only to master and negate difference' (2011: 105). He says that this results in 'a fetishisation of simultaneity and a failure to conceive of the knowledge produced through durational, collective interaction as anything other than compromised, totalising and politically abject' (2011: 105). I would argue that rather than *fetishising* simultaneity, Nancy recognises the significance of these moments of sharing or 'un-working', rooted as they often are in durational collective interaction. Nancy is not dismissing the kind of interactions that Kester refers to, but he addresses the limits of communication within a given community, which is where these radical moments of commonality occur. For Nancy, a limit exposed by communication, is not a 'place', but rather it is the 'sharing of places, their spacing' (IC 1991a: 73). In this way, their logics and intentions are actually much closer than Kester gives him credit for. At the same time, the '*sharing* of places' allows for dissonance, more specifically, recalling Mouffe and Laclau, a kind of dissonant engagement that aims to respond to others in this space, rather than attain an ideal outcome. Nevertheless, Nancy's philosophy questions the idea that dissonant engagement might lead to a new hegemony, instead drawing attention to how such engagement might exceed the hegemonic.

However, Kester later asks an important question: '*How do we determine which forms of insight, and which efforts to destabilise existing systems of meaning, are liberating or empowering, and which are harmful or destructive?*' (2011: 113: emphasis added). This question concerns the political. Although Nancy's approach facilitates the continual reconfiguring of the limits in a way that allows for greater multiplicity and freedom, he recognises the need for structure. In *The Birth to Presence*, he states that although reason is appropriative, *irrationality* is 'more appropriative than reason itself, for it is so by annihilation' (1993: 180). We need rationale: principles and logics that determine which forms of insight are empowering and which are destructive. However, both Kester and Nancy highlight the need to address *how* these are determined. Part of the determining process is to allow for the continuing discernment of forms of insights, whether these are harmful or liberating, and this requires the opportunity for people to engage *with* the 'determining authorities'.

The process of determining which forms of insight have meaning has long been dominated by the single narrative of globalisation, a narrative that has reinforced and perpetuated inequalities and led to ecological crisis. Hailing a 'new climatic regime', Latour forwards the concept of 'the

Terrestrial'. This shift draws attention away from both the illusory horizon of the Global and the fantasy of the Local, instead refocusing on how we relate to, and engage with, the earth.

In her essay 'Outlining Art: On Jean-Luc Nancy's Trop and Le plaisir au dessin' in the *Journal of Visual Cultures*, writer Ginette Michaud explains how, for Nancy, art allows us to see and respond to the ways in which we are *part of* the world. She reminds us that for Nancy the process of mondialisation (perhaps synonymous with becoming Terrestrial) is itself an art and that '[a]rt is not seen as being a representational relation to the world, but as offering us nothing less than access to this world' (Michaud 2010). In this sense, we are required to respond creatively, with thought and care, to other agents, human and non-human. Michaud explains, 'We understand today that a world is . . . a milieu in which we find ourselves and which we can only perceive from the inside . . . everything it implies of the order of knowing and mastery ceases to be dominant or overviewing' (2010). She uses 'within' to describe our relation to the world, implying a sense that we can never 'disconnect' from it. Consequently, what we 'know' ceases to be knowledge of the 'the whole', because we are 'with' the world and not beyond it.

Having established 'being singular plural' as 'first philosophy', Nancy develops the idea of 'being with' from the initial developmental stages in social awareness, through to 'being with' in a political sense. 'Being with' the world, part of the process of 'worlding', part of the process of nature, allows us to focus on the earth itself and how we engage with it. Nancy's detailed and ontological analysis of the conditions for interaction 'with' allow for a deeper understanding of this kind of engagement.

The idea of 'being with' ties in with Nancy's quasi-ontology of 'being singular plural'. Therefore, to adequately address the transformative potential of such creative projects demands a detailed study of how this philosophy works throughout the development of a creative project from its initial formation, to how it is shared and transformed through broadening engagement. This simultaneously requires attention to how the ontological philosophy of being singular plural refers to shared distancing of individual bodies. Nancy's writings, as will be considered, address the significance of 'being with' – he explores how being is synonymous with appearing – that we unavoidably appear *with* others and that this shared co-appearing is what constitutes community. Throughout his writings Nancy conceptualises community as 'inoperative', in that it concerns being together in a retreat from a fixed identity, rather than in the formation of a fixed identity or 'togetherness'. This interpretation of community is key to understanding world-forming as the dynamic being together of bodies constituting the world, which can take place, as I have hypothesised, through the creation of images of the world. In this sense, images are the by-product of the process of being together. Nevertheless, as Nancy invokes in *The Creation of the World*: '[o]ur task today is nothing less than the task of creating a form or a symbolisation of the world' (2007c: 53). However, the significance of this task is in 'being together' as separate bodies that share a distance, rather than in the representations themselves.

Working with Nancy's choices of language, the next chapters explore active, ontological processes. I begin by tracing the development of Nancy's concept of 'spacing' from that of an individual, to spacing of a collective identity (in this case an 'art activist' group). Chapter 3 will chart the progression of Nancy's idea of 'being singular plural' towards its political affect. Subsequent chapters will develop this 'incline' towards political engagement in more depth and with reference to Nancy's gestures of 'exscribing' and 'co-appearing' before culminating in an analysis of how art interventions can enable us to recompose the image of the world.

Note

1. A form is understood as a 'ground that withdraws' (M 1996: 32).

3   Participatory Art
and 'Spacing'

This chapter centres on the performance group Liberate Tate, an art collective that was instrumental in flagging up the ethical issue of oil sponsorship of the arts. The group undertook disobedient interventions within Tate galleries over a period of six years, aimed at severing links between Tate and the oil companies that were sponsoring it. As a participant, I reflect on how Liberate Tate embodied Nancy's ontology of being singular plural through a focus on the idea of 'spacing'. 'Spacing' concerns the nature of 'being' – in particular the shared sense of being 'separate'. My analysis centres on the way in which communicative strategies unfold within and beyond Liberate Tate. Attention to subtleties within these strategies provides an applied understanding of 'spacing'.

The concept of 'spacing' is key to Nancy's writings on being singular plural – a way of thinking that destabilises, and diverges from, phenomenological interpretations of being. In *The Inoperative Community* Nancy writes of 'singular beings' that are 'themselves constituted by sharing, they are distributed and placed, or rather *spaced*, by the sharing that makes them *others*' (IC 1991a: 6). Beginning with Nancy's writings on ontology, this chapter explores how Nancy's concept of 'spacing' relates to ideas of communication and community.

Focusing on 'spacing' allows me to look at how a revised understanding of ontology, as non-phenomenological, can pave the way for engagement with 'the political' that facilitates 'recomposing the image of the world'. Furthermore, I address the themes of 'spacing' and 'communication' through participation in the performances of the art group Liberate Tate. My analysis explores the possibility that a sense of complicity in a creative process can allow us to 'recompose the image of the world'.

Liberate Tate: Politically Engaged Art Practice

Why Liberate Tate? For a long time, I have been interested in how artists and artworks can intervene in cultural discourses, generate a sense of accountability and suggest alternative approaches to specific micro-political issues. Over time, I became more aware of how such artworks can be absorbed into the art industry, and their potentiality reduced. As such I became particularly interested in art collectives that engaged directly with galleries and museums with the aim of reforming the institutions themselves – a process that I believe has significant repercussions in terms of the way in which artworks are 'framed' in cultural spaces, and their wider social significance. These collectives – including the Guerrilla Girls, Superflex and Voina – embodied critical and creative practices that resided both within and outside the perceived boundaries of the art world. Through my research into art activism and collaborative art groups, I came into contact with a member of Liberate Tate who I interviewed in 2013. Having grown accustomed to the familiar BP logo throughout cultural spaces in London, the interview had a big impact on me and I joined the group. I felt that it was important to extend my research further, and approach these themes though embodied practice rather than as a detached onlooker. Although other groups in London, such as Platform and Greenpeace, also generated discourses around oil sponsorship of the arts, I was particularly inspired by Liberate Tate – by the way in which it was explicitly an 'art collective' and did not differentiate between aesthetic strategies and political strategies. In this way, the group moved beyond the aesthetics/political divide that characterised (and still characterises) so many approaches to art interventions.

In 2010, Tate commissioned a workshop exploring art and activism. They invited the Laboratory of Insurrectionary Imagination to lead the workshop. A few months previously, the 'Lab of ii' had been dropped by the Nikolaj Contemporary Art Centre in Copenhagen because they had encouraged 'mass disobedience' during the Copenhagen Climate Summit. As Lars Kwakkenbos states in his article 'Art, Activism, and Permaculture', the group exists 'somewhere between art and activism, poetry and politics' (Kwakkenbos 2011), orienting collective action around friendship.

The workshop focused on the question: 'What is the most appropriate way to approach political issues within a publicly funded institution?' The participants collectively decided to address the issue of sponsorship – specifically BP's (formerly 'British Petroleum') sponsorship of Tate. Subsequently, Tate attempted to censor the workshop, a gesture that intensified the oppositional energy within the group. A majority of the participants then decided to continue the creative collaboration independently from the gallery, ending the workshop by placing the words 'ART NOT OIL' in the windows of the top floor of the gallery. This was the starting point for Liberate Tate who, six months later, performed an 'oil spill' at the Tate Britain Summer Party. The performance featured two women 'spilling' bags of oil-like molasses, hidden under their flowery dresses, as well as a larger 'spill' at the visitor entrance, undertaken by other members of the group.

Like the Lab of ii, Liberate Tate resists categorisation as 'activists' and prefers to be understood as a collective of performers and artists. They act within a larger coalition entitled 'Art Not Oil' which includes other activist, art and performance collectives including Platform, Shell Out Sounds, Greenpeace, the Reclaim Shakespeare Company, Rising Tide, the UK Tar Sands Network, and BP or not BP? who communicate and act collectively to oppose sponsorship of cultural institutions by oil companies.

I joined Liberate Tate in 2013 and my participation has informed the following chapter. Because Liberate Tate performances have, over the years, included more than 500 performers, the 'boundaries' of the group are constantly in flux. To respond to the fluctuating levels of participation, the group distinguishes between those who are 'in the room' and those who are 'out of the room'. To identify a person as 'in the room' is to acknowledge that they regularly attend meetings and co-organise group activities on an on-going basis.[1] These activities include performances, presentations at universities, assisting with workshops and participating in discussion events to which the group is invited and communicating with other groups in the Art Not Oil coalition. When referring to specific instances of participation, times when I was 'in the room', I identify as part of Liberate Tate, using 'we' and 'our'. However, there are points in the chapter, where I either refer to performances prior to my joining the group, or times at which I was 'out of the room' and these are indicated through referring to the group as 'they', to acknowledge my proximity and non-involvement in those instances. On the whole, however, I refer to the group as a separate identity in and of itself, taking care not to overstate my participatory role, even though it influences the way in which I reflect on and respond to other members of the collective.

To effectively generate public awareness, Liberate Tate is required to have a strong collective presence, but at the same time the group does not want this presence to be assimilated and dismissed. Because Liberate Tate is an art collective, its potentiality lies in the creation of images. As Nancy explains in the first pages of *The Ground of the Image*, the image is 'the distinct' – it is sacred and set apart (GoI 2005: 1). Accordingly, the creation of new images concerns the process of setting apart. As such, the group's presence embodies an amplified experience of shared separation. How might the 'shared separation' evoked in Liberate Tate performances recompose the image of the world?

Spacing and Singularity

The obliqueness of art is what constitutes something as 'art' and characterises 'the problem of art': 'The singular plural/singular is the law and the problem of art', Nancy writes, 'as it is of "sense" or of the sense of the senses, of the sensed sense of their sensuous difference' (M 1996: 13–14). This absent singularity – a singularity that is just around the bend – means that art remains ungraspable even as we can sense it. How does Liberate Tate embody this kind of relation, even whilst creating a graspable and clear political message? And how might such an embodiment 'force the movement of the world' (M 1996: 18)? One particular performance epitomises the way in which the singularity of art has the ability to 'isolate or force the movement of the world' – the 2012 performance *The Gift*.

On 7 July 2012, over a hundred Liberate Tate performers offered a 'gift' to the Tate. The gift was a 16.5 m, 1.5 tonne artwork: A wind turbine blade installed in the Tate's Turbine Hall. The artwork, a direct reference to renewable energy sources, drew attention to BP's sponsorship of Tate. As with any donated art, Tate was obliged to discuss the donation at board level. A few months after the intervention, Tate declined the artwork and offered to have it recycled. Liberate Tate collected the wind turbine blade from a storage unit in London and returned it to Wales. Although I did not experience this performance firsthand, I feel that it exemplifies the disobedient and interventionary character of the group's performances. Watching footage of this performance had a strong effect on my perception of the group prior to my participation – it made me more aware of the complex dynamics of creative interventions.

Liberate Tate's *The Gift* was a gesture in which the offering of a gift had a rupturing effect: The act of offering became intensified as a movement of arriving, rather than of having arrived. The process of intervening was sudden and unexpected – a spacing 'where the strangeness of a singularity [was] concentrated' (BSP 2000: 8). And this intervention was shared with a large number of performers and a large audience. Unlike previous performances, the identity of the group remained ambiguous or un-obvious – the participants did not wear black clothing or black veils. As such the performance had a greater sense of abruptness and antagonism.

How does this artwork epitomise 'the problem of art'? In other words, how does the singularity of this performance remain ungraspable whilst generating a particular sense of the world? Granted, there is a clear political goal in the performance – to flag up and criticise oil sponsorship of the Tate and to lobby Tate to cut ties with BP. This can be understood as a deconstructive gesture – Liberate Tate do not advocate for a new agenda; they aim to liberate the gallery from an existing agenda. The group has an antagonistic presence within the gallery, generating a space for critical thought. Whilst the political goal is specific in one sense, it opens onto ambiguity. The group is often challenged by those who ask: 'What do you propose instead?' The answer to this is not within the remit of the group – they are

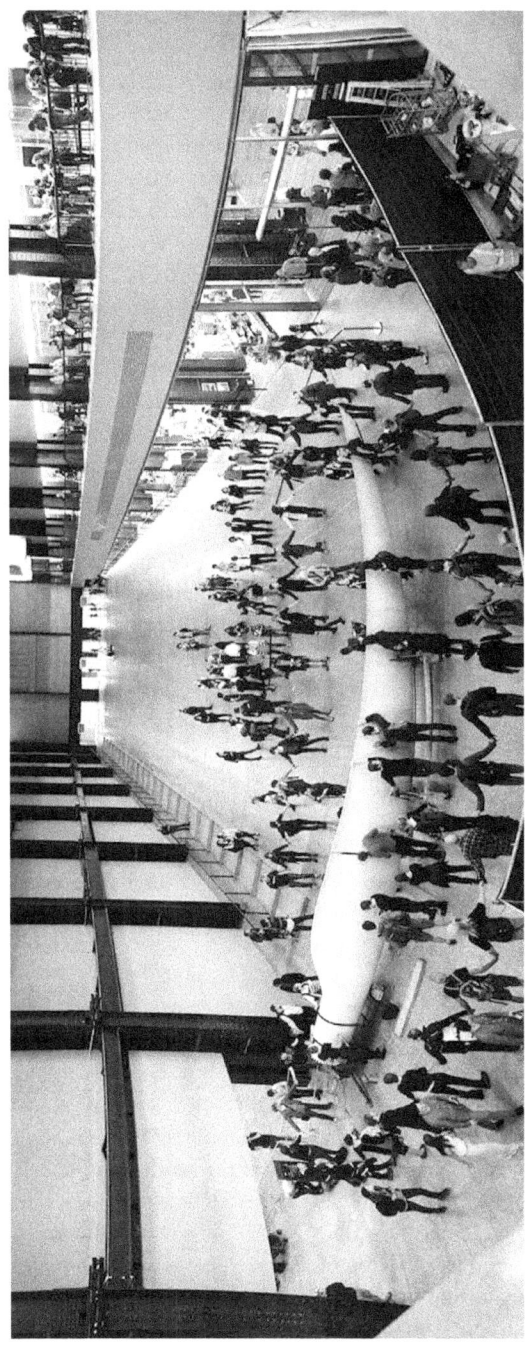

Figure 3.1 Liberate Tate, *The Gift* (2012)

Source: © Ian Buswell

happy for their actions to be simply deconstructive, disrupting discourses to allow for new ideas and approaches to develop.

This ambiguity, and perhaps the sense of an alternative being 'just around the bend', is amplified through the fact that these performances are *art* performances and not 'traditional' protests. Art presents the 'exteriority and exposition' that constitutes the world. This exteriority and exposition is a condition of being, but art *presents* it and demands that we become aware of this *sense* of exposition, even if we might not articulate it in specific terms. In the case of *The Gift* – one of Liberate Tate's more antagonistic performances – the wind turbine blade appears as an external presence, an uninvited gift within the controlled gallery space. The performance took advantage of the clauses within Tate policy that allowed this performance to be legal. More importantly, however, the performance arrests the attention of audiences and reveals ways in which this cultural space resists open discourse, the ways in which those in power use the cultural prestige of an art gallery to influence visitors through advertising (and green-washing) a fossil fuel company.

As Nancy writes, 'Art isolates or forces there the movement of the *world* as such' (M 1996: 18). Here we see that Liberate Tate literally forces their presence into the Turbine Hall, changing the experience of the staff and gallery visitors, shifting perceptions of the gallery. It is through sense, experience and perception that we compose the image of the world, images that characterise our environments. Liberate Tate forces, or isolates, an event within Tate that disrupts an existing sense of the gallery and of BP. This disruption, although micro-political and offering no alternative, affects perceptions of cultural spaces and familiar brands. This is not futile because such gestures incrementally alter the way we think about the world around us, gradually shifting our focus onto political issues (environmental issues) that have been purposefully obscured, to generate a sense of urgency.

Art as Exteriority

As discussed, Nancy writes of 'exteriority and exposition of a being-in-the-world, exteriority and exposition that are formally grasped, isolated and presented as such' (M 1996: 18). Nancy quickly clarifies the meaning of 'being-in-the-world' in this context – 'being-in-the-world' is synonymous with 'being-*of*-the-world' (M 1996: 19). Nancy is keen to emphasise that we are singular plural and therefore part of the world (and constituting the world); we are not separate subjects *within* the world. As considered in the last chapter, Nancy's quasi-ontology allows us to think beyond traditional phenomenology, expressed through the dualism of subject and object, and to understand how being is a state of shared separation, of shared exposition. This is communicated through his use of the word 'spacing'.

For Nancy, art is 'formal' and 'discrete', it is a 'patency' (M 1996: 34). In other words, art is 'open' and unobstructed. It is through this patency, this openness, that art is always in advance of signification, answerable only to itself. As stated earlier, art is the presentation of presentation, the presentation of 'spacing'.

Art practices embody this exposition, both through the creative performance of making an artwork, and through the way in which audiences and participants engage with art. Making a deconstructive political gesture through art, rather than through traditional means of protest, calls for different engagement. It calls for attention to how we are 'of-the-world', how we can embody a patency that makes space for social change.

The appearance of *The Gift*, as an uninvited, inappropriable and external force, dislocated normal social dynamics within the Turbine Hall. As Liberate Tate slowly wheeled the turbine blade into the gallery, one security guard attempted to stop them by lying down in front of the blade. In this extraordinary moment, this representative of the gallery embodied a traditional gesture of dissent and protest against Liberate Tate. At the same time, one member of Liberate Tate calmly repeats to him 'this *is* happening, this *is* happening'. The performance had the force of an exteriority that could not be stopped – it was a performative exposition. As such, in a theoretical sense, the performance 'force[d] there the movement of the *world*' (M 1996: 19), because it altered the dynamics of the gallery and the behaviour of those in the gallery. In addition, it isolated a power dynamic, critiquing it through a kind of joyful antagonism.

Tate, as the focus (and space) of this antagonism had limited options – they could either decline the artwork or they could accept it. Either way, the artwork would sustain the presentation of exteriority and exposition. In the case of it being accepted, the artwork would sustain the disruptive presence of Liberate Tate, it would stand out against the BP-logo-imprinted walls, pointing to and critiquing Tate's ethics. Or in the case of it being declined, as it was, the turbine blade was ejected from the space. Although this rendered the artwork temporal, it is recorded in gallery paperwork and shared by Liberate Tate through video documentation. The absent artwork remains as part of the Tate archive and is catalogued as part of art history. What is the significance of this record? How are such art practices recorded when they situate themselves as outside of the art institution? The next section looks at Nancy's idea of 'cataloguing' in this unique contemporary context.

Cataloguing in a Digital Age

In 2006, Nancy's follow-up book to *The Muses – Multiple Arts: The Muses II* – was published in English. Again, the book is a collection of essays on art, more specifically on the processes of art, including 'making' and 'cataloguing'. In the essay 'Catalogue' in *Multiple Arts: The Muses II*, Nancy writes about how the catalogue produces the 'conditions for visibility' (2006: 149). The essay is a close analysis of François Martin's 1979 exhibition in Amsterdam: *The Air Show*. Consequently, Nancy's analysis stems from attention to the traditional exhibition catalogue, although he does suggest that a catalogue can exist in a minimal form of a list of titles (2006: 149). The following paragraphs, however, will draw on Nancy's essay 'Catalogue' to consider cataloguing in the contemporary context of Liberate Tate performances and the group's use of social media. Interpreting these performances in the light of Nancy's essay requires understanding that Nancy's writings on painting revolve around the idea that painting 'presents' the world, so that his analysis is relevant for all images – painted, photographed or performed – regardless of their form.

As 'disobedient interventions' each Liberate Tate performance is temporal and requires documentation. However, aside from the archival record of *The Gift* – a formality for the gallery – the performances remain largely undocumented within the art institution. Nevertheless, these interventions are 'catalogued' in a way that continues to give them visibility – through the Liberate Tate website and through press coverage and social media platforms. These forms of cataloguing allow Liberate Tate to maintain a dynamic position both within *and* outside the art institution. This section argues that digital technology enables Liberate Tate to catalogue its work in such a way that it continues to have an antagonistic and incommensurable presence within the art world. It suggests that Liberate Tate is therefore able to intentionally embody a constantly renewing relation to the political, a relation that prevents its work from being subsumed and shut down. The group's intention to sustain a critical openness within an arts institution is paradoxical because intentionality is fundamentally a phenomenological concept. Here, however, I am suggesting that critical openness requires a certain kind of intentionality. Just as Philip Armstrong refers to the way in which Nancy's writing touches 'on or *at* the very limits of the phenomenological tradition' (2010: 18), here I am suggesting that political art practices touch on the limits of intentionality, where intent opens up onto the non-phenomenological and requires audiences to let go of phenomenological thinking.

For writer and researcher Emma Mahony, Liberate Tate 'operates at an interstitial distance' from Tate (Mahony 2017: 126). In her essay 'Opening Spaces of Resistance in the Corporatized Cultural Institution: Liberate Tate and the Art Not Oil Coalition' in the *Museum and Society* journal, she looks at how the group maintains an 'interstitial' or 'internal' distance from the Tate. Mahony comments that, from this distance, Liberate Tate (and the ANO coalition) 'open up spaces of resistance ultimately capable of rewriting the cultural sector's corporatised value system' (2017: 126). For Mahony, Liberate Tate is an example of a collective that adopts a 'negotiated moving position' between two approaches – reformation from within an institution and self-government outside of the institution (2017: 132). It is this 'moving position' that allows Liberate Tate to create distance or space within an institution.

Returning to Nancy's writing on cataloguing – he considers how artworks are not founded on the spaces that support them; instead artworks 'partition' themselves off and in doing so, they 'slice into' the space supporting them. Nancy rarely writes about institutions directly, and here his focus is on the articulation of space that happens through the 'partition and distribution' of painting. Nevertheless, this has implications for exhibition spaces, and in this context Nancy's language helps us visualise how Liberate Tate 'slices into' the cultural institution of Tate, creating what Mahony describes as 'spaces of resistance'. Just as for Nancy, partition and distribution allow visibility; these spaces of resistance allow for a renewed visibility of the workings of an institution. He writes: 'The catalogue enumerates the incisions that are primarily an enumeration of the space they divide. Vision is itself dependent on this act of division. Although the existence of the catalogue may diminish ad infinitum, it will never be reduced to nothing' (2006: 150). Cataloguing work – naming it, sharing it, documenting it – makes visible the ongoing act of dividing and affirms artworks as incommensurable.

How does Liberate Tate catalogue its work? Works are named during group meetings prior to each performance. Each intervention is recorded by a film-maker and a photographer. There is a social media team, who immediately disseminate photos and messages through Twitter and Facebook. Prior to each performance, participants are briefed to use the same hashtag, to ensure a cohesive and concentrated presence on social media. The group often invites journalists from newspapers and media sources – for example, *The Guardian*. At times, we have been joined by journalists from other countries who are documenting global climate change activism. Video documentation is one of the most important aspects of cataloguing Liberate Tate's work, as it communicates with audiences directly and affectively (this chapter will later look at how the group communicates in a 'contagious' way). With the declining popularity of printed news and the increased use of online news platforms, video footage has become central to how mainstream media sources cover Liberate Tate performances. This is further enabled through video-sharing platforms such as Vimeo and YouTube.

The immediacy and apparent transparency of video documentation amplifies debates around corporate sponsorship and fossil fuels, and these debates quickly proliferate through Twitter and Facebook and on the comments section of newspaper articles. Mahony comments on the significance of social media and press coverage: 'The success and longevity of the counter public spheres Liberate Tate create in response to their actions is greatly assisted by the extensive press coverage they illicit and the parallel debates they inspire on social media platforms' (2017: 137). Even 'negative' responses, for example, critical responses by the columnist and Turner Prize judge Jonathan Jones, serve to magnify Liberate Tate performances. However, as comments and opinions spread, the language used to describe these performances can shift and begin to reframe the artworks as simply 'protests', glossing over the more complex dynamics at play.

Cataloguing and Social Networks

In their book *The New Spirit of Capitalism*, Luc Boltanski and Eve Chiapello critically examine the ever-changing structures that sustain capitalism, especially acknowledging the ways in which creative practices and countercultures are often subsumed into capitalism, thus creating this 'new spirit'. Although the book was published in 1999, prior to the proliferation of social media platforms, Boltanski and Chiapello address the role of networks in sustaining the empiricism that is necessary for capitalism to flourish. Writing of the 'radical empiricism' of networks they comment: 'Rather than assuming a world organized according to basic structures . . ., it [radical empiricism] presents a world where everything potentially reflects everything else: a world, often conceived as "fluid, continuous, chaotic" [referencing Vincent Descombes], where anything can be connected with anything else, which must therefore be tackled without any reductionist aphorism' (1999 [2005]: 144). Even 21 years later, we can see this manifest in references to 'fake news' and the way in which this phrase is used with relation to capitalist agendas and right-wing populism. Nevertheless, social media continues to evolve in ways that demonstrate self-awareness regarding the complexity of networks and the way in which this fluid connectivity can be absorbed and instrumentalised by capitalist agendas.

Boltanski and Chiapello comment on how in Anglophone literature, world-views 'based on network logics attached themselves to pragmatism and radical empiricism' (1999 [2005]: 146). As such it often seems that activists and artists, in fighting against or trying to transform capitalist connectivity, actually sustain what Boltanski and Chiapello describe as the 'new spirit of capitalism'. But what if an individual or a group develops self-aware and critical engagement with network logics whilst still engaging with them? Creative activist groups are increasingly aware of the ways in which open spaces are quickly subsumed or instrumentalised and, rather than fighting this sublimation, they embrace it in a way that shifts focus onto the temporal affectivity of communication. One way that campaigns often do this is by having multiple 'messages'. Often global justice movements flag up a number of different issues. This is not to say that such interventions lack focus, rather that they have multiple focal points and platforms, and can shape a number of different political discourses. In this way, campaigns can look beyond the networks of capitalism and engage with them in a way that knowingly challenges the status quo. There can be an acknowledgement that practices will likely become subsumed by the spirit of capitalism, but at the same time an awareness of how they might embody a shift in the values that characterise capitalism, allowing for spaces of antagonism to open up within it. In the introduction to *The New Spirit of Capitalism* Boltanski and Chiapello write about how 'micro-displacements' allow capitalism to flourish but also cause shifts in its underlying value system, thus 'distancing a larger number of actors and creating new inequalities and injustices' (1999 [2005]: 35). These shifts sustain non-capitalist practices and, over time, can weaken capitalist networks and lead to larger social changes.

In the context of Liberate Tate, we can observe this shift in the way in which the views of art critic and journalist Jonathan Jones changed over time. Initially Jones was an advocate for fossil fuel sponsorship, clearly stating that in the light of cuts in funding, '[i]f they can get money from Satan himself, they should take it' (Jones 2010). Seven years later, after Tate and BP ties were cut, he reflected: 'It is blind and narrow for arts organisations to pretend they are outside the struggle to save nature' (Jones 2017). Here we can see a huge shift in values – Jones acknowledges the environmental and cultural significance of oil sponsorship, and rather than prioritising art institutions as he did previously, he looks at the bigger social and ethical picture. Nevertheless, he closes the article with the words: 'It is not true that you can cut off a source of money to museums without harming art. Without BP there might be no portrait award. So let's tell it truthfully: in the interest of the planet, art will just have to lose face' (Jones 2017). Here we can see a return to a capitalist logic that affirms a particular value to art. Instead of embracing the creative evolution of art practices and institutions – one that can be fossil free – Jones returns to the more pessimistic view that art will be compromised without such forms of sponsorship. But in the process of this articulation, in communicating a capitalist argument from a different underlying value system, we can nevertheless begin to see how a shift in the status quo can open up new conversations and possibilities for social change that no longer conform to capitalist logic. These processes of communicating and interfering remain outside capitalist frameworks, and enable the dismantling of elements of capitalism, slowly eroding it or altering it from within. The focus on the process of social network*ing*, rather than on the outcomes of social networks also amplifies the ways that information spreads and modifies – leading to a sense of communication as a kind of unpredictable 'contagion'.

The New Spirit of Capitalism suggests that the artistic critique should 'take time to reformulate the issues of liberation and authenticity, starting from new forms of oppression it unwittingly helped to make possible' (Boltanski and Chiapello 1999 [2005]: 468). And it can do this by slowing down practices and processes so that there are fewer 'tests' and 'abandoning a quest for liberation defined as absolute autonomy' (1999 [2005]: 469–470). This would require recognition of others (and by default being Other) and engagement with what has previously been understood as external authorities and institutions. I will return to this idea in Chapter 4. Importantly, Boltanski and Chiapello state: 'the renewal of the artistic critique notably takes the form of an alliance with the ecological critique' (1999 [2005]: 472) – something we can see embodied through Liberate Tate performances and their knowing engagement with social networks.

Spacing and Communication

Having acknowledged the significance of social media, particularly in terms of cataloguing work, I now return to the idea of communication in a more general sense. My aim is to reexamine the way in which communication is understood not only in terms of social media but through observing and participating in collective action. This section looks at communication with relation to Nancy's quasi-ontology and the writings of Georges Bataille.

In the preface to *The Inoperative Community*, Nancy says that we should dismiss the idea that messages are 'transferred'. Rather, we should understand that 'in "communication" what takes place is an exposition: finite existence exposed to finite existence, co-appearing before it and with it' (IC 1991a: XL). Communication exposes a limit, and Nancy describes this limit not as a specific 'place', but rather as the 'sharing of places, their spacing' (IC 1991a: 73). That is to say, communication exposes the shared exposition of finitude (spacing), which highlights the incommensurability of the other, and in doing so counters the possibility of ultimate unification or consensus.

Referring to the idea that 'clear' consciousness (a consciousness that is on such a 'limit' of being-with-self) takes place as the communicat*ing* of community (rather than 'is' a communication), Nancy, in an important footnote, further clarifies what he means when he speaks of 'communication' (IC 1991a: 19). He aligns himself with Georges Bataille, who stresses the 'violence' done to the word 'communication' and with Derrida's deconstruction of the word in *Signature, Event, Context*, and emphasises its 'untenability'

(IC 1991a: 157). For Nancy, 'communication' essentially refers to the process of transmitting itself, rather than a transmission of a comprehensible message. In his own words, Nancy 'superimposes' the word 'sharing' onto 'communication', and this overlaying of meaning is crucial to understanding how communication relates to 'spacing' (IC 1991a: 157).

Communication can only happen in a community; it is conditional on 'being-with'. And Nancy clearly states that community necessarily coincides with being: 'Community is given to us with being and as being, well in advance of all our projects, desires, and undertakings. At bottom, it is impossible for us to lose community' (IC 1991a: 35). If we understand that being is necessarily 'with', we understand that we are always part of a community. The idea of 'community' is often idealised – being 'part of a community' is something that many people feel is a choice. However, for Nancy, the plurality of being means that we are always part of a community, regardless of how we interact with it. For example, one might choose *not* to engage with the community they live in, but this choice is manifest as a communication to others in the community, and does not exclude the fact that however one behaves, they are still an accountable presence within the community.

For Nancy, finitude exists as communication, as the 'compearance' or 'co-appearance' of each subject's finitude (IC 1991a: 28). Communication is the exposition of finitude, the sharing of finitude. This sharing articulates difference and defines each singularity. Consequently, Nancy understands community as defined by a process of 'mourning'. By co-appearing, each singularity manifests incommensurability and finitude, which spotlights distinctions and detachment. However, this *shared* consciousness of how being singular plural is characterised by separation and loss, connects and affirms a community (IC 1991a: 29, 30). Following this train of thought, we might understand that at the root of community is a sense of loss, an 'unworking' (IC 1991a: 39) brought about by both the finitude of communication and the communication of finitude.

Nancy says that we should not stop 'letting the singular outline of our being-in-common expose itself', because when singular beings share and expose their limits, they 'escape the relationships of society' and are 'unworked' in community (IC 1991a: 41). That is, within the sharing of finitude, of a coming loss, each singularity is open to the 'space of play of the world', and can sustain critical distance from fixed social categorisations. One way of doing this is through emphasis on the exposure, rather than transfer, of meaning in communicative processes. The following paragraphs explore the idea of communication as a shared separation – spacing – with reference to Liberate Tate.

Nancy draws on Bataille's use of the word 'contagion' as an alternative word to 'communication'. Bataille understands contagion as a kind of affective communication. In his essay 'Bataille and the Birth of the Subject' (published in *Angelaki*), Nidesh Lawtoo explores the formation of the subject with relation to what he calls 'Bataille's career-long meditation on contagious forms of mimetic communication' (2011: 44). Lawtoo emphasises that this contagious communication is not necessarily verbal, but that it is a moment in which a spacing 'subject' becomes part of a 'communicative flux' in which the division of the self and other is blurred or transgressed (2011: 74). Examples of this might be contagious laughter, being moved to tears by another distressed person, and can be as ordinary as a contagious yawn. But there is always a sense of excess in this communication, a sense of transgression or overstepping. It is the release of rationality, the moment at which one spaces oneself from their ontic self and 'expends' oneself. And for Nancy, the concept of communication as contagion underlines how spacing and communicating is a shared separation.

Additionally, 'contagion' is completely unpredictable, and this 'accidental' nature of communication is important to bear in mind when considering Nancy's interpretation of the word and the concept of 'spacing'. As in an epidemic, a contagion appears as an eruption or outbreak. It is something that is entirely 'other', but that manifests itself *with* an individual. In this way, it 'spaces': it is indeterminable, able to modify. Contagion pervades populations in an erratic way, which is why it is so difficult to bring under control. However, this irrationality poses a vital question when we understand it in the context of communicating. For Nancy, irrationality is more appropriative than reason because it appropriates though annihilation (BtP 1993: 180). So we need to ask: How might the haphazard nature of contagion shape political discourses? Should we (and if so, how) regulate the ways in which irrational appropriation influences political decisions? These issues underpin the conceptualisation of Nancy's incline from ontology to politics, and the idea of regulation will be addressed in more detail in Chapter 5 with relation to evaluating art.

Liberate Tate often embody an exaggerated sense of this shared separation, for example during small workshops that sometimes form part of the group's monthly meet-up. During one meet-up, we were scheduled to have a creative session to generate ideas for possible installations and performances. Prior to the discussion, the member of the group leading the session asked us to take part in an exercise. We each had to choose two other people in the room, without disclosing their identity. The idea was that each of us must remain as far away as possible from the first person, and as close as possible to the second. For the duration of the exercise (approximately 3 minutes), the group formed a shifting, disrupting jumble. Each person's actions were 'contagious' in that the movement of one person immediately triggered the movement of each member of the group, as they rearranged themselves in accordance with the game.

The exercise highlighted the fact that the togetherness of a group is *made up* of such tensions; the push and pull between singular beings. The exercise encouraged participants to embrace this exaggerated sense of 'shared separation' and to feel more confident to share creative ideas, without necessarily wanting to have a final consensus. This process made us aware of the developing 'thereness' of the group and the shared spacing of each being, and to perpetuate a 'space of play' within the group. The game made me more aware of the necessity of tensions within the group discussion that followed, and allowed me to be able to withdraw, critique and develop ideas collectively. Moreover, I was aware that this critical distance was something that was shared with each member of the group.

A Summary: Spacing and World-forming

In *The Creation of the World or Globalization*, Nancy states:

> In any case, the decisive feature of the becoming-world of the world, as it were . . . is the feature through which the world resolutely and absolutely distances itself from any status as object in order to tend toward being itself the 'subject' of its own 'world-hood' – or 'world-forming'.
>
> (CoW 2007c: 41)

World-forming is the quasi-ontological becoming of the world. Nancy's quasi-ontology is an approach to being that recognises the edges of phenomenological thinking. Nancy instead asks us to focus on what it means 'to be' or 'to become', and considers presence as a 'taking place' or as an active coming-to presence. Here, the appearance of a presence is the appearance of a shared separation, paradoxically the appearing of disappearance – a spacing. As such, Nancy's concept of appearing is developed from the ontology of being singular plural, and not from phenomenological appearing.

Nancy reminds us that although the world has no origin, it is not *lacking*. He says 'the being of the world is the thing permeated by the nothing', and that 'there is no longer a thing in itself but rather the transitivity of being-nothing' (CoW 2007c: 69). And for Nancy, the absence of an origin, of an established point of certainty, is at the centre of the idea of creation and creating. Being-nothing is a *transitivity* – it is characterised by transition, by spacing. The 'transitivity of being-nothing' differs from phenomenology in that it lacks intent (toward a particular outcome). However, there is a paradoxical logic within Nancy's quasi-ontology, which becomes even more evident when explored through an art practice, in this case with Liberate Tate: Inoperativity requires work. Because the group fails to 'work' within a larger apparatus, it creates space for critical engagement. Participation in Liberate Tate performances suggests that without 'intentionally' sustaining these non-functional spaces of critique, creative practices are more quickly subsumed into capitalist networks. Such 'intentionality' is non-phenomenological because it is not intent toward a particular object, but away from a thinking that is oriented around the subject/object. Instead, the work of continuing to suspend appropriative thinking can allow creative practices to flourish. In turn, as such practices flourish, the underlying values of larger institutions can shift and spark social change.

In Nancy's 2016 book *The Disavowed Community* (a book in which he returns to a discourse with Blanchot that began 30 years earlier with Blanchot's *The Unavowable Community*, and which also draws upon Bataille's understanding of community), Nancy clarifies this paradox further, describing such work as 'less unworked than devoted to its unworking – this makes a big difference' (DC 2016: 74). What might this look like in a wider curatorial context? Does this idea of unworking have relevance for institutions? Developing a reading of Nancy with relation to cultural practices and institutions, may initially seem at odds with Nancy's thought because he rarely refers to intentionality, agency and institutionality. Nevertheless, Nancy's philosophy is not itself entirely inoperative; his writings unfold and 'work' within cultural discourses. They have concrete significance because they can help sustain 'inoperativity'.

As this chapter has discussed, this paradoxical 'intentionality' can become manifest through acknowledging how communication is 'contagious' – that it affirms the shared separation that constitutes being. For Nancy, 'contagion' indicates the 'passion of a singularity' – the 'excess' of a singular being that corresponds to the sharing of singularity (IC 1991a: 32). Understanding communication as contagious not only spotlights the shared separation of being, but also emphasises the way in which communications alter and modify through the process of communicating – to communicate is not simply to transfer meaning, because meaning shifts through the process of communicating.

In highlighting strategies of creative engagement, both within the group itself and through its methodology in the gallery space, this chapter has explored how practitioners can pose questions and open up new possibilities for engagement with established institutions. In this sense, it has begun to address the key term 'recompose', with a focus on the latter fragments of this term – 'compose'. The word 'compose' has layers of meaning. Its initial root is the Latin *pausare* 'to cease, lay down' and 'pause', which is derived from the Greek *pauein* 'to stop, hold back, arrest, to cause to cease' – indicating an interruption. As outlined in this chapter, Liberate Tate's interventions create a rupture in institutional logics that deem it acceptable to use cultural space to provide advertising for fossil fuel companies. They 'interrupt' an ordinary sequential logic. They also generate a break in the expected experience of the gallery-goer. These performances 'arrest' the attention of the viewer and create a temporary 'pause' in the familiar mechanics of power within cultural spaces. However, this only provides the founding sense of the term 'recompose'. To extend this further, the next chapter will look at the second sense of 'compose' – the Old French *composer* meaning to 'put together, arrange, write' a work – in this case, how meaning is 'put together' in a curatorial project.

Notes

1. These activities include performances, presentations at universities, assisting with workshops and participating in discussion events to which the group is invited and communicating with other groups in the Art Not Oil coalition.

4 Contemporary Art and 'Exscribing'

'Exscribing' refers to how sense is exposed – to the way in which sense constitutes, but exceeds, materiality. It is a concept that extends throughout Nancy's philosophy to focus attention on how consciousness simultaneously interprets the world and carries itself beyond interpretation. This chapter considers the political relevance of 'exscribing' alongside my involvement with the London-based collective Art Action UK (AAUK),[1] a small group of artists, curators and writers who organise an annual residency along with exhibitions and discussion events that address the political issues that have arisen following the 2011 tsunami and nuclear meltdown in Fukushima, Japan.

In his essay 'Exscription' in *The Birth to Presence*, Nancy says: 'Writing, reading, I exscribe the "thing itself" – "existence", the "real" – which *is* only when it is exscribed and whose *being* alone is what is at stake in inscription' (BtP 1993: 338, 339). Later in 1997, in *The Sense of the World* Nancy develops the idea of exscribing to address the 'thought of the sense of the world':

> a thought that, in the course of its being-thought, itself becomes indiscernible from its *praxis*, a thought that tendentially loses itself as 'a thought' in its proper exposition to the world, a thought that *exscribes* itself there, that lets sense carry it away, ever one step more, beyond signification and interpretation.
>
> (SoW 1997: 9)

To exscribe is to articulate a reality, but to exceed it at the same time. Like spacing, exscribing is a prerequisite for what 'is'. Both 'spacing' and 'exscribing' refer to a simultaneous process of bringing some*thing* into being whilst being conscious of, and sustaining engagement with the way in which this is happening. However, the word 'exscribe' focuses attention on how thinking carries sense 'beyond signification', and how consciousness at once interprets the world and carries itself beyond interpretation. *The Sense of the World* is a key text for this chapter, but I also continue to reflect on and respond to earlier texts in *The Birth to Presence*, tracing ideas through to Nancy's 2015 book *After Fukushima: The Equivalence of Catastrophes*. The fragment '-scribe' refers to the action of writing. Nancy's use of '-scribe' is a philosophical reference to Derrida's concept of 'écriture' and as such it signals the dislocation of meaning that takes place through writing. Nancy often uses the word 'inscribe' in his writing to indicate a relation to a 'trace'. For example, in *The Birth to Presence*, he writes of how we might 'inscribe the trace of a name' and he refers to how the limit of finitude 'inscribes itself' (1993: 57). The idea of a trace indicates Nancy's engagement with Derrida's texts *Of Grammatology* and *Signature, Event, Context*. Although these texts will not be analysed here, further contextualisation will be found in the next chapter where I go on to discuss how the concept of the trace influences Nancy's writings on 'retracing' or 'the retreat'.

A prefix to '-scribe' indicates a relation to the act of writing. The prefix 'de-', whilst it is generally used to indicate position (down, down from, off), also carries with it a weighting towards totality (down to the bottom, totally). Similarly, '*in*scribe', which means to 'write on or in', carries with it a focus on writing into a surface drawing attention to the object receiving text. *A*scribing again carries a different nuance – the prefix 'as-', an assimilated form of 'ad-' from the Latin 'ad', indicates being 'to' or 'towards' something. *A*scribing consequently carries a sense of attributing or assigning something to a pre-existing thing or pattern. Conversely, the prefix 'ex-' of exscribe indicates a movement 'out-of/from'. It forms the basis of words such as *ex*istence, *ex*teriorisation, *ex*pulsion and *ex*cess. Nancy's writings on ontology are based on the idea of existence as a state of being 'thrown' into the world and he emphasises this motion 'out-of/from' – the idea of something exceeding, moving quickly beyond a boundary. Although Nancy often uses the word 'inscribe', this chapter will focus on the term 'exscribe' and its opposite, 'ascribe'. The concept of 'exscribing' relates closely to the quasi-ontological framing of 'world-forming'.

In *The Birth to Presence* Nancy writes of 'exscrip*tion*': 'Writing, and reading, is to be exposed, to expose oneself to this not-having (to this not-knowing) and thus to "exscription"' (BtP 1993: 338). He explains that writing exposes meaning, but that we are left with this exposition. Suggesting the 'clumsy' articulation of the word 'exscripted' to indicate writing that has been 'discharged' by its own meaning, he says that the word 'exscripted' 'exscribes nothing and writes nothing' but indicates the process of writing from the 'uncertain thought of language' (BtP 1993: 338). The noun 'exscription' points to the evidence of exscribing, rather than the process. Because I am exploring the process of 'world-forming', I will focus on the verb 'exscribe' and the action of 'exscrib*ing*'. I hope that this will emphasise the intended 'incline' of analysis, stemming from Nancy's interpretation of ontology with its attention to the dynamic relation between ontology and the ontic. The idea of exscribing as a process that lacks nothing, and yet is incommensurable, is key to the analysis that develops throughout this chapter.

I consider the political relevance of 'exscribing' alongside my involvement with the London-based collective AAUK. AAUK provides a platform for artists who tackle political and philosophical questions relating to nuclear energy production. The group does not directly take part in 'activist' strategies, although it potentially provides a space for artworks that do. What is the social significance of an arts group that is politically powerless? And what effect can AAUK have socially? My role in the group – providing write-ups of talks, performances and events for the website, managing social media pages and co-curating an exhibition – will enable me to further explore the concept of 'exscribing', and will begin to consider how a small arts organisation can affirm and underline the political significance of 'exscribing'.

This chapter continues to explore the idea of power, and responds to Carl Schmitt's conceptualisation that 'the state of exception' is an opportunity to define a new norm. To question this idea, it interprets political power as something that is never 'fixed' but is contingent on the duality between emptying and regulating power. It compares Nancy's use of the word 'exscribing', particularly in *The Sense of the World*, with Schmitt's use of the word 'ascribing' and his sole focus on 'ascribing meaning', by turning to Paolo Virno's writings on communication as a 'constantly renewed deferral' (2008: 60). By comparing Virno's interpretation of the biblical concept of the 'katechon' to the oscillation between ascribing and exscribing, it argues that these two concepts are simultaneous and coexisting.

It will also discuss how 'exscribing' relates to our understanding of 'the political'. Nancy understands the political as 'an incessant tying up of singularities with each other . . . without end or structure' (SoW 1997: 111–112). This approach is challenging because it does not define or prescribe a particular political ideology. Instead, in *After Fukushima: The Equivalence of Catastrophes*, Nancy directly refers to political discourses post-Fukushima to highlight the need for an approach to politics based not on 'general equivalence' but on 'common incommensurability' (2015: 41). I argue that this approach to political discourses can be found within cultural practices, but needs to be further supported and encouraged within established organisations.

This chapter focuses on art practices that challenge and disrupt the feeling of having 'made sense' of the world. Such disruptions are important because they prevent 'appropriative thought': thought that balks against the unknown and retreats into praxes which reinforce existing social narratives that continue to privilege some groups of people above others. To value the process of reaching, of 'sensing', is to acknowledge the human condition of 'being singular plural'. By articulating the way in which sense and materiality coincide, this chapter focuses on the mid-point of the incline from ontology to politics – the point at which our responses to the ontology of 'being singular plural' become manifest within wider social discourses and begin to characterise our engagement with political issues. Nancy's writings draw attention to the agency we have within the process of 'worlding' and the importance of sustaining connections to practices that influence and reform social paradigms.

Exscribing and Sovereignty

After the earthquake and tsunami in East Japan in 2011, AAUK initially raised money for the international relief programme through charitable events: art raffles, art auctions and food stalls. These events raised small sums of money throughout 2011 for organisations such as the Japanese Red Cross and World Vision. However, after some consideration, AAUK decided to focus on creating an on-going, independent residency project that would allow artists who lived and worked in Fukushima to have respite away from the disaster area. The residency provides an annual opportunity for artists to come to the UK to continue their art practice in a new environment, and to communicate the on-going social and political issues following the disaster to new and unfamiliar audiences.

Kaya Hanasaki was Art Action UK's first artist-in-residence. Her residency took place in London in May 2012, just 14 months after the earthquake. Her artworks aimed to problematise the governmental response to the disaster and to consider the political climate of Japan within a wider social context. Although Hanasaki's work did not explicitly address 'sovereignty', it touched on themes that relate to 'the state of exception' and created a sensory experience that reflected concerns about the power dynamics of political policy-making.

Hanasaki's residency artwork *Portrait in Mask* was a socially engaged artwork – she asked participants to each wear a surgical mask and to have a photographic portrait taken. Although in many parts of the world wearing a mask is commonplace – for example, if one has a cold – at this time in 2012 (prior to the Covid-19 pandemic), most of the London-based participants would have been unfamiliar with wearing a mask. Hanasaki wanted participants to have a heightened awareness of their own breathing. She wanted

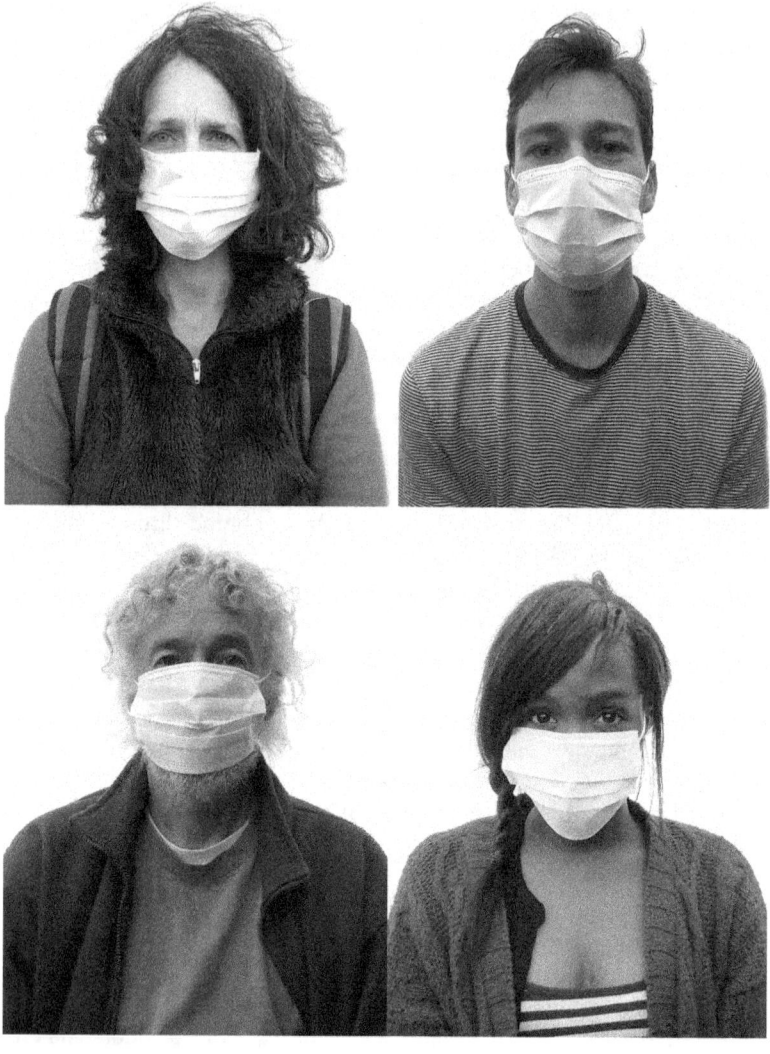

Figure 4.1 Images from *Portrait in Mask* (2012)
Source: © Kaya Hanasaki

to generate a sense of empathy towards those who, living in irradiated areas of Japan, were at risk from contaminated air. She felt that, in Japan, in the months following the earthquake, those who wore masks demonstrated distrust of the government's safety guidelines. In some cases, those wearing masks were verbally attacked (Grainger 2019).

A few weeks before Hanasaki's residency, the Japanese government had released new nuclear safety standards. Although a poll in July 2011 had shown that the majority of Japanese people (74%) wanted Japan to become nuclear-free,[2] the government had proposed revised safety laws on the nuclear reactors. This new legislation specified that nuclear reactors would have a 40-year lifespan, which could be extended. This legislation paved the way for further nuclear developments. Even though the government made gestures to restore public confidence, through increased testing and monitoring, they were not willing to decommission nuclear plants.

Following the disaster, more people began to openly criticise the Japanese government, some spotlighting the ways in which the crisis, and the crisis management, was bound up in capitalist agendas. The same year as Hanasaki's residency, New York-based Japanese writer and translator Sabu Kohso wrote the essay 'Turbulence of Radiation and Revolution' in which he states:

> All conduct of the Japanese government in the wake of 3/11 has proven that the state would choose continuation of capitalist operation and its own sovereignty over the well-being of the people. It has been constantly blurring information about present risks of radiation and critical conditions of the power plants.
>
> (2012b)

Like Hanasaki, Kohso articulates how capitalist values have prevailed over democratic values. The same year (2012), Kohso wrote another essay, 'Radiation and Revolution', in which he describes how the human body has become 'a battleground over the commons' or an 'informational front' in which concepts of commonisation are not just side-lined, but under attack from capitalist ideologies (2012a). As widespread opposition to nuclear technology continued during this year, a stronger focus on 'transparency' aimed to reassure the general public (for example through a live video stream of the Fukushima Daiichi Nuclear Power Plant) and the government was able to ratify the continued development of nuclear technology.

How do artworks such as Hanasaki's *Portrait in Mask* criticise and challenge the power and sovereignty of the government? As an anti-nuclear activist, how might Hanasaki's artworks during the residency relate to global audiences? First, it is necessary to consider the role of sovereignty with relation to 'the state of exception'. Second, it is important to reflect on Nancy's question at the end of his essay 'On Sovereignty' in *The Creation of the World or Globalization*: 'And if sovereignty was the revolt of the people?' (2007c: 109).

The State of Exception

Political theorist Carl Schmitt understood the state of exception as a state of emergency declared by the sovereign. Here, the state of exception does not refer to the emergency itself, but to the theory of state that articulates a situation as 'an emergency'. This articulation involves the codifying of an exception that lies beyond the existing legal order – a process that re-writes 'the norm' (Schmitt (1934) 2005 edition: 6). It is this process of codification that, in Schmitt's writings, actively creates a monopoly to decide, which in turn affirms the sovereign as such. Here we see a logic that tries to assimilate the external exception and use it to create a new rule.

On the other hand, philosopher Giorgio Agamben understands the state of exception as 'a space devoid of law' and as a 'zone of anomie in which all legal determinations are deactivated' (2005: 50). He argues that although Schmitt understands the state of exception as outside of the law, he tries to inscribe[3] it within the law, whilst acknowledging its separateness. If the state of exception is 'used' as a rule, it self-negates and can no longer be an exception. Instead it is used to wield power and define what is normal and what is not. Agamben says that this ultimately creates 'a killing machine' such as National Socialism (2005: 86).

Rather than inscribing the exception within a new rule, Agamben believes that the state of exception should always be outside of the juridical order.[4] At the end of his book *State of Exception*, he concludes that 'the only truly political action . . . is that which severs the nexus between violence (understood here as the "use of power") and law' (2005: 88). In other words, by inscribing the state of exception within law, as Schmitt does, a 'nexus' is created. If we visualise the nexus as a kind of 'tie' or connection, the act of 'severing' it would surely require a specific decision, a gesture of violence that would break the connection rather than undo it. Nancy's understanding of the political offers an alternative response. For Nancy, politics is 'an incessant tying up of singularities with each other . . . where the tie is taken up again, recast, and retied without end, nowhere purely tied or untied' (SoW 1997: 111–112). We can compare this concept of a connection, which is neither complete nor incomplete, to the nexus between a destructive force and a regulatory force (violence and law). The word 'incessant' is vital and highlights Nancy's unique approach to the distributing of power. Whilst Schmitt tries to *secure* a nexus, Agamben tries to *destroy* the nexus. But neither addresses the duality of *any* response to a state of exception – that a 'nexus' between destructive and regulatory forces can neither fully exist nor be fully destroyed. Nancy, on the other hand, acknowledges that an 'exception' will automatically be assimilated into a shared reality, but at the same time he recognises that this shared reality is part of an infinite 'enchainment', a 'tying up of singularities with each other' (SoW 1997: 111–112). The 'incessant' process of the tying/retying of a nexus means that the connection is never entirely fixed. However, to prevent the artificial concept of 'a norm' from becoming a dominant and prohibitive influence on the 'tying up of singularities', this permanent lack of fixity can be spotlighted.

The previous chapter addressed Nancy's question 'And if sovereignty was the revolt of the people?'[5] (CoW 2007c: 109). Sovereignty was understood as a social relation that must be reinforced by the people to remain powerful. Therefore, if the people cease to recognise sovereign power during a state of emergency, this relational paradigm is abandoned and the state of exception is confirmed as external to the juridical order. Here we begin to invert Schmitt's theory of state, because by exposing the emptiness within power, the people sustain the external nature of the state of exception.

However, being outside of the juridical order *of the state* is not the same as being outside of a fundamental inclination towards justice, towards jurisprudence in a wider philosophical sense. But, when declared by the people, the concurrent tension between a destructive emptying of power (violence) and the creation of regulations (law) is more evident. This exscribing of power is as an empty*ing* of power, rather than an emptiness *within* power. But power does not vanish – it becomes re-appropriated by the people. Singularities tie and retie, but people have access to this process and can expose the temporality of the social relation that constitutes the sovereign, thereby sustaining the possibility for new political ties.

The idea of sovereignty as the revolt of the people does not equate to populism. Populism, and particularly right-wing populism is often oriented around the sovereign power of individual leaders, and the desire to define and affirm what is 'normal'. Ece Temelkuran, in her book *How to Lose a Country: The Seven Steps from Democracy to Dictatorship*, explains how the 'populist leader paralyses the political mechanisms while gradually invading the state apparatus. Party and state become one, the leader needs state powers, yet they disintegrate whenever he needs to evade criticism' (Temelkuran 2019: 157). Here we can see how populist movements are often led by individuals who paralyse the political mechanisms that allow for democracy, so that ultimately the people affirm, rather than 'empty', the power of this individual, becoming more powerless in the process. Temelkuran points out: 'The habit of imagining our institutions as powerful, abstract beings, and forgetting that *they* are actually people who might be too paralysed to react, is a classic failure when grappling with authoritarianism, even for the executives of those very institutions' (2019: 157). In this book, I am approaching the idea of the institution through a reading of Nancy's philosophy of being that is pre-institutional. Although this might seem paradoxical, the aim is to renew our thinking of institutions and to focus attention on the ability of institutions to listen, respond to and adapt through democratic processes. By approaching institutions as social structures that are always called on to make new decisions, we can begin to appreciate that even established institutions are 'pre-institutional' in that they are constantly forming and responding. As Temelkuran points out, populist leaders achieve power through the dismantling of institutions. As such, this book forwards an approach to social change that requires engaging *with* institutions.

Returning to Kaya Hanasaki's *Portrait in Mask*, we can begin to understand that the gesture of wearing a mask does not just signify a private decision to protect oneself. It is a public sign of mistrust in state assurances. It communicates this scepticism to others. It provokes a shared sense of doubt that can quickly proliferate. This public manifestation of insecurity discredits the authority of the government. Although each individual decision to wear a mask seems insignificant, it becomes a collective gesture of opposition – one that exposes the creation of a new 'norm' to justify a political decision.

Although this may not immediately trigger a tangible political response, it transmits an international message. For example, by creating and exhibiting *Portrait in Mask* in London, asking UK audiences to wear a mask, Hanasaki draws attention to the way in which political decisions regarding energy production can quickly impact and endanger fundamental human rights, such as breathing uncontaminated air. Her work not only elicits an emotional response, it is a reminder of the need for 'the people' to exercise their free will in order to challenge capitalist political logics over energy production. Discussing these issues in London in 2012 highlighted connections between Hanasaki's anti-nuclear activism and the demonstrations against the use of nuclear power and nuclear missiles in the UK. *Portrait in Mask* tries to undermine belief in the capability of state mechanisms, not just in Japan, but in all countries that are developing nuclear technologies.

Ascribing and Exscribing

Although the Art Action UK residency programme foregrounds artists who live and work in East Japan, the group organises and participates in events and exhibitions that feature other international artists, especially artists exploring issues around nuclear energy production. In March 2015, I co-curated the AAUK exhibition and event series *Those Who Go East* with artist and curator Kaori Homma at White Conduit Projects in London. White Conduit Projects is a project space in North London featuring the work of Japanese artists and designers alongside international artists. It opened in

2014 and, following interest in AAUK, the gallery director Yuki Miyake offered the use of the project space for free, particularly because *Those Who Go East* commemorated the fourth anniversary of the earthquake and tsunami. Alongside Japanese artists, the exhibition and panel discussions provided a platform for UK artists who have 'gone east' to the irradiated areas to make art, as well as artists who live in those areas. *Those Who Go East* featured a screening of The Otolith Group's 'The Radiant',[6] Chris Wainwright's photographic images from the devastated area of Kamaishi[7] and a discussion with artist Kirk Palmer about his video works based on the lingering presence of the atomic bombings in contemporary Japan.[8]

One of our goals was to create a sense of a shared international dialogue around nuclear energy production. What became evident in the talks that accompanied the exhibition is that British artists have a creative challenge: Such site-specific and 'political' artworks need to acknowledge the 'foreignness' of the artists, whilst exploring global concerns *with* local people. Each artist wanted to create an aesthetic experience that was led by the space itself; an experience shared with, and guided by, those who experienced the disaster and its consequences first hand. The artists wanted to open up opportunities to question and discuss the politics at stake within the spaces featured, rather than to communicate an opinion or ascribe a specific meaning. Does this ambiguity or indecision mean these artworks are ultimately apolitical?

Returning to Schmitt, he argues in *Political Theology: Four Chapters on the Concept of Sovereignty* that the purity of a legal idea can never be realised. He says that every legal thought brings a legal idea that 'needs a particular organisation and form before it can be *translated* into reality' (Schmitt (1934) 2005 edition: 28–30: emphasis added). Here the formation of a concrete idea requires an authority that decides on how to conclude a juristic act. This is a process of translation, a process of 'carrying across' in which the 'pure idea' alters according to the translator's perception and communicative decisions. In this case the 'legal thought' brings with it a 'legal idea' and the sovereign decides on how to translate the idea into a reality.

This sovereign decision ultimately 'emanates from nothingness' (Schmitt (1934) 2005 edition: 31). Schmitt extends the idea of the juristic decision as a 'translation', and begins to speak of it as a point of 'ascription' that determines normative behaviour: 'Ascription is not achieved with the aid of a norm; it happens the other way around. A point of ascription first determines what a norm is and what normative rightness is' (Schmitt (1934) 2005 edition: 32). For Schmitt, the juristic decision requires attributing the exception to a particular cause in order to create a new norm. In the context of continued nuclear energy production in Japan for example, many people believe the Japanese government has focused on attributing the consequences of the nuclear disaster to a force majeure (rather than inadequate technologies installed in an area in which there are frequent earthquakes) in order to reinforce the perceived necessity and normality of nuclear technologies. Schmitt refers to Marxism to explain how the point of ascription can provide a systematic basis for political and social changes (Schmitt (1934) 2005 edition: 43). But he critiques Marxists for finding the 'point of ascription' in the economic sphere, where value is relational. However, the reinforcement of any specific 'systematic basis', even one based on non-economic ideals, has repercussions that can destabilise democratic politics.[9] A focus on creating what Schmitt calls a 'point of ascription' allows those in power to hold on to their sovereignty – to monopolise power and minimise or disregard the concerns of those with less power.

However, if we consider the possibility that sovereignty could be 'the revolt of the people', the point of ascription is no longer the focus of the interplay of power because sovereignty is evident through the *emptying* of power (even as it re-ascribes it). Here the significance of 'exscribing' becomes predominant. In his early writings in *The Birth to Presence* Nancy says that '[t]hought exscribes itself, it corresponds to *itself* (as it must to be what it is) only in this outside of itself to which it alone remits (or rather, emits, and throws, and abandons)' (1993: 176). To exscribe thought is to carry it beyond signification and interpretation. Exscribing 'abandons' what has been posited as 'normative rightness'. By focusing on the way in which thought 'performs itself' as 'a thought', we acknowledge that something 'precedes thought in thought itself' (BtP 1993: 176). Exscribing goes beyond the original 'point of ascription' and although it ultimately ascribes a new thing, the focus is on the transformability of these points rather than their permanence.

How can art, which necessarily ascribes meaning to materials and actions, also illuminate the way in which it simultaneously exscribes meaning, and why might it do so? As part of *Those Who Go East*, Kirk Palmer discussed his photographic and video works. The photographic series *Precious Fragments* documents places within a one-kilometre radius of the hypocentre of the atomic bomb in Nagasaki. These images try to revive a sense of places that were devastated in the nuclear bombing. The title *Precious Fragments* is a reference to memories that arise spontaneously (an expression used by cognitive psychologist Marigold Linton). The images have a mysterious quality; they appear to 'reside between an ambiguous historical time', no longer anchored in the present moment (discussion on 14 March 2015). Palmer emphasises that his artworks are personal attempts to reflect on the atomic bombings, but that these are *shared* reflections. He wants to create spaces that facilitate a process of contemplation and expressly wants

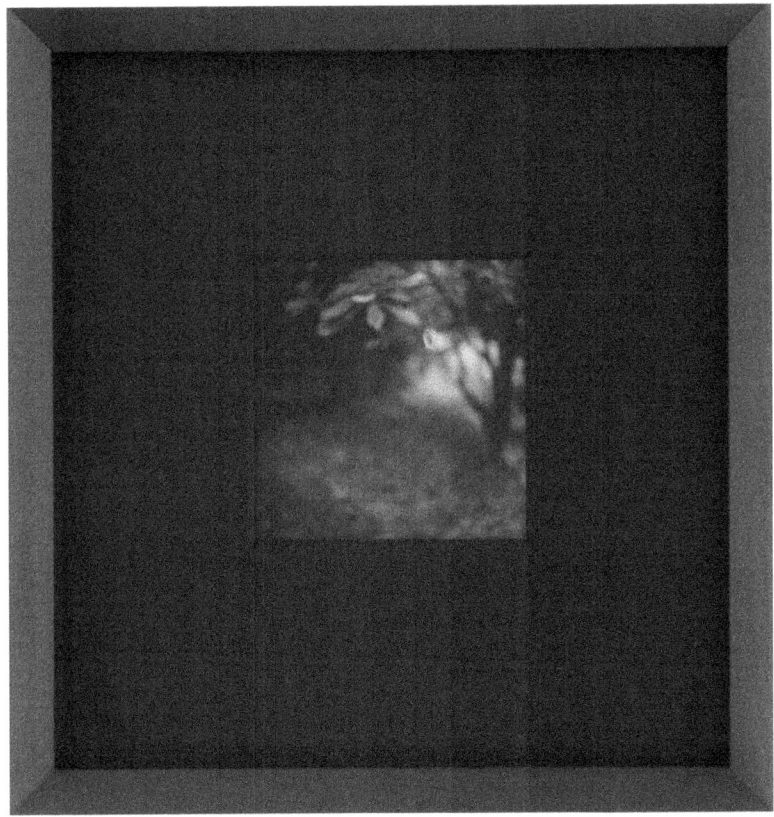

Figure 4.2 Image from the series *Precious Fragments* (2014), b/w selenium toned silver gelatin hand print

Source: © Kirk Palmer

to avoid 'telling' viewers what to think. 'The works are quite open in a sense that people can bring their own knowledge, thoughts and feelings about those events to the works', he explains (discussion, 14 March 2015). The video works provide a space for contemplation in which audiences can uncover and exscribe their memories through a process of meditation. Palmer does not have a concrete political goal. 'I'm representing the space that allows people to make their own observations and enter into the work in a similar way to me', he explains. 'It's an empathetic process. It's impor-tant that lessons are learned [from the bombing], but part of that process is first of all feeling something and then setting about understanding it as well as you can' (discussion on 14 March 2015). By prolonging the sensing that takes place prior to our ascribing meaning, a potentially transformative space is created. Deliberate attention to how we exscribe sense, to how sense is beyond interpretation, can lead to changes to the wider social consciousness or particular issues and the way in which we respond to them. This requires a suspension of pre-formed narratives and images, an emptying of the mind that enables the viewer to 'sense' the spaces featured in the artworks.

Nevertheless, exscribing and ascribing are concurrent; exscribing always brings about a concrete thing that is part of the tangible world. Each artwork, and each thought of an artwork becomes part of 'an order' – part of a reality. Nancy states that 'to compose is to regroup, reintegrate, return, reduce' (BtP 1993: 325). Creative processes reorder the way in which we sense the world, but if we seek solely to ascribe meaning in these processes, we ultimately begin to reduce sense. If, however, we are aware of the impermanence of meaning, of how signification is generated through both ascribing and exscribing meaning, we remain open to sense.

Exscribing as a 'Political Task'

So far, this chapter has explored how Nancy's concept of exscribing relates to sovereignty and has looked at the ways in which ascribing and exscribing characterise engagement with art. It has highlighted the ways in which cultural practices influence how we sense the world, and how we conceptualise this sense. It will now address how acknowledging 'exscribing' might influence our perception of the political.

In his essay 'Political Writing' in *The Sense of the World*, Nancy explains that writing does not pass on 'a sense' of something, but it '*makes sense in being passed on and shared among individuals*' (SoW 1997: 118). Although writing exposes an absence of signification, the relation between presence and absence and a shared sense of a message is important. For Nancy, the 'political task' is 'to let the relation as sense "ground itself" in the signification of being together "as its figure". Only on this condition – that the "relation" should be a "figure" – can the *together* of the group avoid the alternative between *all* and/or *nothing*' (SoW 1997: 119). To let 'sense "ground itself"' requires a passivity that paradoxically arises from an intentionality towards non-intentionality' (D 2008: 52). This is a decisive consciousness of, and criticality towards, how one senses the world and requires us to cultivate a kind of enduring passivity. Here, passivity does not mean a complete refusal to have opinions, or a refusal to make decisions – it means not clinging to these as fundamental truths. Even when making and carrying out daily choices, this passivity can characterise the sense of the world and the way in which sense is shared with others (recognising that it is singular plural).

For Nancy, writing is political because it traces out 'the essencelessness of relation' rather than an 'effect of an "engagement" in the service of a cause' (SoW 1997: 119). It is political because it facilitates a shared communication in which sense grounds itself differently each time, rather than being contrived through pre-formed strategic goals. Because the significance of the communicative bond lies in its incommensurability and its ultimate failure to 'serve a cause', communication also requires a suspension of certainty.

However, even if (as with AAUK and Liberate Tate) there are no 'final' or conclusive goals, there are smaller goals along the way and these are articulated through a decision-making process. Whilst Nancy recognises that decision making is necessary, he focuses on our relationship to meaning, to how we reach our decisions and our level of attachment to them, rather than the meanings that are ultimately reinforced through each decision. Ten years after writing *The Sense of the World*, Nancy returns to address the political task before us. One of the key passages quoted in this book is from *The Creation of the World or Globalization* where Nancy says that our task is

> nothing less than the task of creating a form or symbolization of the world. . . . It is the extremely concrete and determined task – a task that can only be a struggle – of posing the following question to each gesture, each conduct, each *habitus* and each *ethos:* How do you engage with the world?
>
> (CoW 2007c: 53: emphasis added)

The following paragraphs will consider engagement with the world with reference to how we exscribe the 'in-common' of existence and how this has temporal significance.

Writing has a communicative role. It accentuates our ontological condition of being singular plural and opposes the 'cutting-up of the world into exclusive worlds' (SoW 1997: 119). Here we can begin to understand that by representing something – through gestures, speech, text or art – we engage in the *process* of communicating. Communicating acknowledges the non-exclusivity of individual worlds. It is the recognition of the plurality of existence, and even though each communication fails to entirely capture a sense of a reality, we share an awareness of this failure. It is this awareness of an absence that binds our being-in-common. This is why Nancy says that existence 'decides itself as a certain *in* of the in-common' (SoW 1997: 93). Existence is characterised by the shared awareness of the difference that we have in common.

When sovereignty becomes the revolt of the people, it does not mean that power evaporates. The idea that the people can 'exscribe' sovereignty (as they re-ascribe it) emphasises the political as the place of 'being together'. But Nancy, in an essay entitled 'Politics I' in *The Sense of the World*, warns that 'the becoming-truth of the political can go so far as to absorb sense into itself' (SoW 1997: 89). For 'the political' to function and acknowledge plurality it must ultimately remain ideologically non-objective, a political engagement that requires passivity and receptiveness towards that which is not knowable, the Other.

This chapter is focusing on how an arts organisations might respond to the aftermath of a disaster and how this engagement is 'political'. Organisations and collectives often have to articulate how they provide tangible relief, or to show how they function towards a particular end. Following a disaster, when there are pressing issues concerning shelter, healthcare and food, how can an arts collective respond to the 'in-common' of the Other? In such critical conditions, there is still a need to sustain communicative bonds with those affected. Through sustained communicative processes, political ties form in the present, where they do not take the form of goals or ideals to be projected into the future. These communicative processes recognise the importance of being responsive to emotional and non-material requirements, which are often minimised when those in need have few rights.

During the 2014 AAUK artist residency, Haruka Komori and Natsumi Seo shared their video documentaries of communities in Rikuzentakata recovering after 3/11. The documentaries reflect on the abruptness of the Japanese government's response to the disaster. The rebuilding process has been rapid and efficient, but it has prioritised pragmatism. As a result, many living in the area feel that they have once again been disenfranchised because they have not had a genuine opportunity to respond collectively. Although there have been public consultations, often these were held so soon after the initial impact of the disaster that many in the community were still in a state of shock and unable to fully engage with the task of participating in the rebuilding process.

During the Japan Foundation panel discussion, David Alexander, Professor of Risk and Disaster Reduction at UCL, commented on the speed of the recovery programme in Japan. In the past, a recovery programme following a disaster of this magnitude has taken up to 25 years, but the restoration of infrastructure in these areas has already largely been completed. Nevertheless, the psychological and emotional impact of the disaster will have longer repercussions. This is where art has significance. Alexander believes art has an important role in communicating and nourishing the human spirit and he reflected that 'art has answers as much as science'; it reflects a shared *sense* and the experience of reality and can reframe and impact these experiences too (discussion, 14 March 2015).

Nevertheless, in the same panel discussion, Yoi Kawakubo also highlighted that communities have been rearranged and 'almost broken' by living in temporary housing locations. Here we can see the complexity of decision making, even when it is intended to be in the best interests of those affected by the disaster. In his book *The Writing of the Disaster*, philosopher Maurice Blanchot explores how we try to describe and explain disaster and how the incommunicability of disaster affects us. He writes of those who have been 'made passive' through a disaster (Blanchot 1986: 15). On the one hand, many in the community feel disempowered by the government's quick 'utilitarian' response, and on the other hand, many others feel constrained because they are stuck in temporary housing locations, and want the rebuilding process to be even faster. Both viewpoints balk against the sovereignty of the government but are discordant. But in both instances, the government has assumed the needs of those affected.

AAUK endeavours to address these conflicting issues and to highlight the need for local decisions to be made *with* communities, even if this would require a staggered, slower and more articulated process of rebuilding – a process that demands a receptiveness on the part of those with more power. By acknowledging that a disaster is incommensurable, AAUK maintains a sense of the political as a tying and untying of relational bonds, without adhering to a particular structure. In simple terms, although this approach can easily be criticised for its lack of political effectiveness, its purpose is to sustain openness and responsiveness to others, and to preserve a shared sense of freedom. At length, for the group to listen and not simply administrate, it has to respond to 'being-in-common'.

In *After Fukushima: The Equivalence of Catastrophes*, Nancy addresses the incommensurability of singularities through a discussion of the Marxist idea of 'equivalence'. He situates creative processes at the heart of our ability to acknowledge 'non-equivalence'. Acknowledging the Marxist theory of exchange, Nancy reminds us that although 'value' can change, generated as it is through social relations, it subsequently determines an 'exchange value', which is usually expressed in economic terms. Nancy points out that the systems that drive global capitalism (the raw materials required and the organisations needed to implement and sustain these systems) all depend on a 'general interconnection', and this is the idea that they must all lead to profit (Nancy 2015: 5). Nancy discusses how, for Marx, 'the equivalence of money could be demystified in favour of the living reality of a production whose social truth is the creation of true humanity' (AF 2015: 33). Nevertheless, the demand for profit has compounded the exploitation of power and has led to 'a condition of finality' in which 'everything becomes the end and the means of everything' (AF 2015: 36). This helps us understand how capitalist technologies increasingly exert autonomous power over us. This sense of 'general equivalence', Nancy argues, is catastrophic. Because social relations become increasingly expressed through 'exchange values', our experiences and relationships are at risk of becoming reduced to commensurable 'products'. The only way to resist the 'consumption' of reality is to acknowledge and support incommensurability – to recognise and appreciate the distinctive particularities of each person, situation and experience.

The catastrophic nature of such equivalence is exemplified in disasters such as Fukushima. Although every disaster is unique, each disaster connects 'with the totality of interdependences that make up general equivalence', and over time this sense of general equivalence has given rise to the idea that humans can be 'in charge' of the world (AF 2015: 6, 7). However, Nancy believes that Fukushima has added 'the threat of the apocalypse that opens onto nothing, onto the negation of the apocalypse itself' because the use of the atom, whether this is for nuclear power or weapons, dissolves the link between the strong and the less strong in society (AF 2015: 21, 22). It therefore takes with it a relational structure that defines human experience, and the possibility of a politics of the 'in-common'.

By acknowledging the non-equivalence of the disaster, we recognise its incommensurability. We can comprehend how, as Blanchot writes, the 'disaster *disorients the absolute*' and appears as the 'intense suddenness of the outside' which 'comes to us from beyond the confines of decision' (Blanchot 1986: 4, emphasis added). Accordingly, we reinforce the non-equivalence of human existence and the need for consciousness of sense and relationality – a return from the macro-political to the micro-political.

Nancy clarifies the idea of non-equivalence saying that it 'does not overturn equivalence; it makes it explicit. It says: All are equal in that no one is identical or commensurable with others' (AF 2015: 60). How then, do we exscribe the 'in-common' without reinforcing a sense of equivalence? This is an important question for any organisation that is trying to raise money to help people recover from a disaster. Nancy reminds us of the 'naive belief in the possibility of a virtuous handling of general equivalence' (AF 2015: 32). Although realistically money is needed to support and help communities that have been devastated by 3/11, it is important not to see fundraising as 'a solution'. Although AAUK began as a collective that was fundraising for international aid, it recognised the importance of providing space for a deeper critique of the social issues faced by those affected by disaster. The initial fundraising efforts created a sense of social responsibility. But the emphasis on raising money detracted from the overarching aim to provide support and solidarity for those affected. When social responsibility is expressed through the relationship of a financial donation, it can accentuate the difference between the people donating and the people receiving the funds, and eventually amplify a sense of general equivalence.

In *After Fukushima: The Equivalence of Catastrophes*, Nancy reminds us that 'the *present* is the place of closeness – with the world, with others, oneself' (AF 2015: 37). As discussed in the previous chapter, 'spacing' and 'world-forming' refer to the presenting of being, which is synonymous with time. In the introduction to *The Creation of the World*, François Raffoul and David Pettigrew define Nancy's world as an 'absolute immanence' (CoW 2015: 5). World-forming corresponds to nothing other than itself, and like the process of reification, it reveals the transcendental. But its transformative potential to create new political ties rather than reinforce global paradigms depends on our willingness to remain in the present as 'place of closeness' – to have the capacity respond to the world with an openness for the new and unknown. Nancy says: 'What would be decisive, then, would be to think in the present and to think the present' (AF 2015: 37). This thinking of the present is 'decisive' in that it decides, not on some*thing* – a particular goal or future – but on the immediate and responsive decision to be guided by the approach to the singular presence. This increasingly goes against the grain of contemporary technologies and systems, which depend on general equivalences and the 'need' to ascribe value with relation to a future intention.

Nevertheless, this decision to 'think the present' is a natural process. In his discussion with John Paul Ricco in *Art in the Anthropocene*, Nancy suggests that the unexpected is actually the 'regime of the world'. He says that 'we are accustomed to speeds, intensities, quantities or population or energy, that have no equivalent in our past – but we inhabit them, we engage with them raw, we cultivate their own possibilities' (2015: 88). This is particularly evident in the ways in which we have been called to respond to the global Covid-19 pandemic. Writing of the virus in *The European Journal of Psychoanalysis*, Nancy describes it as a 'viral magnifying glass' that 'enlarges the characteristics of our contradictions and of our limitations' ('A Much Too Human Virus' 13/4/2020). A magnifying glass enlarges images, allowing us to become aware of fine details. But at the same time, as history relentlessly beams through this 'viral magnifying glass', we are experiencing a flare of consciousness, a burning awareness of the issues to be faced now, in the present.

Earlier in this chapter I addressed Nancy's appeal to take up the political task of 'posing the following question to each gesture, each conduct, each *habitus* and each *ethos*: How do you engage with the world?' (CoW 2007c: 53). The significance of the task lies in questioning how we sense the world and how we conduct ourselves within it. Within this task is an obligation, not to decide *for* the other but to acknowledge 'being-in-common' and decide *with* the other, an obligation that requires us to be open to the approach of singular beings and their experiences. To pose the question 'How do you engage with the world?' to 'each gesture and conduct' is to invite co-appearance and to demonstrate openness to the world.

The idea of caring 'for the approach of singular presence' (AF 2015: 40) underpins AAUK's residency programme. Nevertheless, there are still decisions relating to the number of art events and fundraising events, the location of exhibitions and the artists participating in the residency, and there is a very fine line between these structural decisions *characterising* the residency and allowing the residency to evolve. These structural decisions involve much negotiation. The final decisions are collaborative and are guided by specific events and opportunities arising each year. The objective of the residency is to allow artists to talk more freely regarding sensitive political issues in East Japan and to give the artists as much freedom as possible. All those involved (there is usually a group of five or six people, including the artist, who are contributing to the organisational process) trust in the success of the residency or exhibition, because beyond increasing support for the group to enable further residencies, there is not a fixed target.

A Summary: Exscribing and World-forming

As discussed in the previous chapter, we experience finitude through 'spacing', because to 'be' is to be 'singular plural'. This is 'world-forming', a creative process in which people reaffirm and form affiliations. Although world-forming – the becoming-present of the world – often reflects and reinforces the global equivalences that characterise 'globalisation', Nancy uses the expression to remind us that the world is always becoming, and that it is the becoming-present of the world that allows for new paradigms to emerge.

This chapter has studied the concept of 'exscribing' – a process that allows sense to 'emerge from finality' and exceed a given meaning even as we ascribe it (AF 2015: 37). The chapter has explored how, as we sense the world, we both ascribe and exscribe meaning. We ascribe meaning to our surroundings but, at the same time, our sense exceeds our understanding of the world.

This chapter has developed the concept of intentionality by highlighting the contemporary political task: to question the way in which we make sense of the world. By acknowledging the indeterminacy of sense, we can reinforce the incommensurability of singularities. To value non-equivalence requires us to resist the inclination to 'conquer' the future and to determine and classify singular beings and events as they appear. Instead it has stressed the need to 'care for the approach of the singular presence' (AF 2015: 40) by being guided by the other in a mutually responsive way. The concrete focus of this chapter has been on the arts collective Art Action UK. It has considered the formation of a state of exception and how we understand and communicate experiences of disaster alongside the analysis of how we ascribe and exscribe meaning. It has suggested that acknowledging the way in which we 'exscribe' meaning, leads to questioning the norms by which a state of exception is defined. Fundamentally, we can only brush against the unknowable, and can only touch on the unrepresentability of the earthquake, tsunami and nuclear meltdown in Fukushima in 2011. Nonetheless, acknowledgement of exscribing allows us to share a sense of absence with others. But this awareness of shared sense approaches finitude in a way that affirms the quasi-ontology of 'being singular plural' and attests to the incommensurability of each individual.

This chapter has reflected on a curatorial project – on how a collection of artworks is 'put together'. As such, it elucidates the second layer of meaning in the term 'recompose' in which the Greek and Latin meaning of the word 'compose' (as an interruption, a holding-back) adapts in Old French *composer*, meaning to 'put together, arrange, write' a work. Here, the idea of an interruption expands to highlight a sense of rearranging, of putting things together. This chapter has looked at how, through exhibitions and events, AAUK 'composes' a new perspective on the disaster and its political implications. This 'rearranged' image of individuals and groups in contemporary Japan counters media- and government-endorsed cultural programmes, providing new perspectives that encourage viewers to thoughtfully engage with artworks. The word 'compose' also overlaps with the Old French *poser*, which carries a sense of pausing and placing, and develops to contain an additional meaning 'to puzzle, confuse, perplex'. This shifting meaning also resonates through AAUK's approach to curating, where the aim is not to articulate a clear affirmative message, but rather to complicate clearly defined ideas and stances.

In his conversation with John Paul Ricco, Nancy reflects that the meaning of 'sense' is 'devoid of purpose, accomplishment – in the sense of fulfilment of purpose and fullness reached – is the most commonly shared sense among us (and perhaps all living things)' (2015: 90). How then can the idea of sense as 'devoid of purpose' relate to co-appearing? It is one thing to analyse the significance of world-forming gestures within an organisation such as AAUK, but how can such gestures be adopted 'formally' within cultural institutions? The next chapter will consider these questions from within an established cultural institution.

Notes

1. AAUK was established in 2011 by UK-based artist Kaori Homma, Tokyo-based sociologist Yoshitaka Mōri and curator Meryl Doney.
2. Nagata Kazuaki, 'Fukushima Meltdowns Set Nuclear Energy Debate on Its Ear', *The Japan Times*, 3/1/12.
3. As outlined in the introduction, to 'inscribe' gives precedent to the thing receiving the inscription – in this case, Schmitt reinforces the 'surfaces' or boundaries of the law from a position of sovereignty.
4. Agamben draws from Walter Benjamin's 1928 book *The Origin of German Tragic Drama* and reflects that 'in deciding on the state of exception, the sovereign must not in some way include it in the juridical order, he must on the contrary, exclude it, leave it outside of the juridical order' (Agamben 2005: 55).
5. In the postscript at the end of Nancy's essay 'On Sovereignty'.
6. Curated and directed by Kodwo Eshun and Anjalika Sagar, the Otolith Group explores archival documentation, sonic communication and the moving image within gallery spaces. *The Radiant* is a film essay that looks at the invisible consequences of the 2011 nuclear meltdown.
7. Chris Wainwright was the lead artist and advisor on a three-year project with Future Lab Tohoku to provide a cross-disciplinary, arts-based contribution to the social rebuilding and cultural enhancement in the Kamaishi area in the Iwate Prefecture of the Tohoku Region of Japan, devastated by the 2011 tsunami and earthquake.
8. Other participating artists were Kaya Hanasaki, Yoi Kawakubo, Kaori Homma, Haruka Komori and Natsumi Seo, and sociologist Dr. Yoshitaka Mōri.
9. For example, speaking with relation to energy politics in *This Changes Everything*, social activist Naomi Klein speaks of 'the underlying democratic crisis that has allowed multinationals to be the authors of the laws under which they operate' (2014: 360).

5   Cultural Institutions and 'Co-appearing'

This chapter centres on Nancy's use of the word 'co-appearing'. Co-appearing spotlights the awareness of how each presence also carries with it a sense of the unknowable, an understanding of appearance that further indicates Nancy's shift beyond phenomenological traditions, discussed in Chapter 2. This chapter addresses the ethical implications of being-singular-plural and of 'co-appearing'. To consider this in concrete terms, I draw from my role as a 'learning assistant' at the Arnolfini in Bristol, particularly throughout the 2016 exhibition *Art from Elsewhere*, a touring exhibition that focused on socially engaged art practices. As a learning assistant, I undertook audience research for the gallery. In this chapter, I actively explore how institutions facilitate co-appearance.

This chapter continues to analyse the central incline of the book – the development of Nancy's quasi-ontology through to political engagement – with emphasis on institutional practices. It considers the gesture of 'co-appearing' with reference to Nancy's text 'The Compearance'[1] and a later text – 'Co-appearing' – in *Being Singular Plural*. Nancy defines 'co-appearing' as 'an ontological gesture of mutual exposition with Others that raises the question of why particular subjects 'appear "together" and for what other depth they are destined' (BSP 2000: 59). Co-appearing generates consciousness of another depth, a sense of absence and of absenting.[2] As Philip Armstrong writes in his essay 'From Appearance to Exposure': 'The positing of what comes into appearance is now remarked not by its substance or self-identity but in and *as* its exposition and exposure, or in and as a *sense* of exposure' (2010: 12).[3] It is this consciousness of displacement, exposure and absence that characterise Nancy's writings on appearing. Again, this understanding of appearance marks Nancy's shift beyond phenomenological traditions – whilst his writings retain a 'close proximity' to phenomenological conceptualisations of being (James 2006: 96). Understanding appearing as exposure to absence distinguishes Nancy's thinking and allows him to diverge from phenomenological traditions. Nancy's understanding of co-appearing as a 'gesture of mutual exposition' is key to thinking of the political as a 'retreat'.

In *Retreating the Political*,[4] the social and political significance of co-appearing is addressed through the idea of a 'retreat'. The retreat is not simply a withdrawal from the certainty of political ideologies; it also demands that we retrace and revise their conditions (RtP 1997: 138). Implicit in the idea of 'retreating' is a collective process of re-creation in which 'appearing with' facilitates the possibility for renewal. This chapter explores how 'the retreat', as a form of critical withdrawal from certainty (from foregone conclusions that adhere to familiar social paradigms) interrupts knowledge and traces new sites for communicating and co-appearing.[5]

This chapter addresses the ethical implications of being-singular-plural and of 'co-appearing'. It explores how an institution can acknowledge and embody social responsibility. As a 'learning assistant' during the 2016 exhibition *Art from Elsewhere* (a touring exhibition that focused on 'socially engaged art practices in a global context', and featured 39 artists from 22 countries), I supported the visitor engagement team by gathering feedback from audiences. Reflecting on this experience, I explore how institutions can facilitate co-appearance through looking at the ways in which institutions 'listen to' and respond to audience feedback.

Having participated in many Liberate Tate interventions, I was keen to look at political art practices from the perspective of an institution, especially one in Bristol – the European 'Green Capital' for 2015. Although oil sponsorship is not an issue with relation to the Arnolfini, I chose this organisation because of its charitable status and because its exhibitions engage with discourses around ecology and contemporary political art practices. In April 2016, the exhibition *Art from Elsewhere* opened at the Arnolfini (and Bristol Museum). Aimed at addressing 'life, politics and identity in a globalised society', the exhibition was conceptualised along seven themes: Borders, Transformations, Violence, Rituals, Surveillance, Resistance and Capital. I volunteered to help with the audience engagement research for this exhibition because I wanted to see how it might facilitate critical and creative engagement with political discourses.

Continuing to develop a reading of Nancy, this chapter responds to the writings of political theorist Hannah Arendt. It considers how the Arnolfini, as a charitable cultural institution, might resist the pressures of neoliberalism. Again, interpreting Nancy's writings in the context of institutional practices may seem discrepant, as the very notion of institutionality runs counter to Nancy's sense of being-towards-the-outside. Nevertheless, I am suggesting that there is a sense of alterity at the heart of cultural institutions, which is why they have cultural significance in the first place. I am

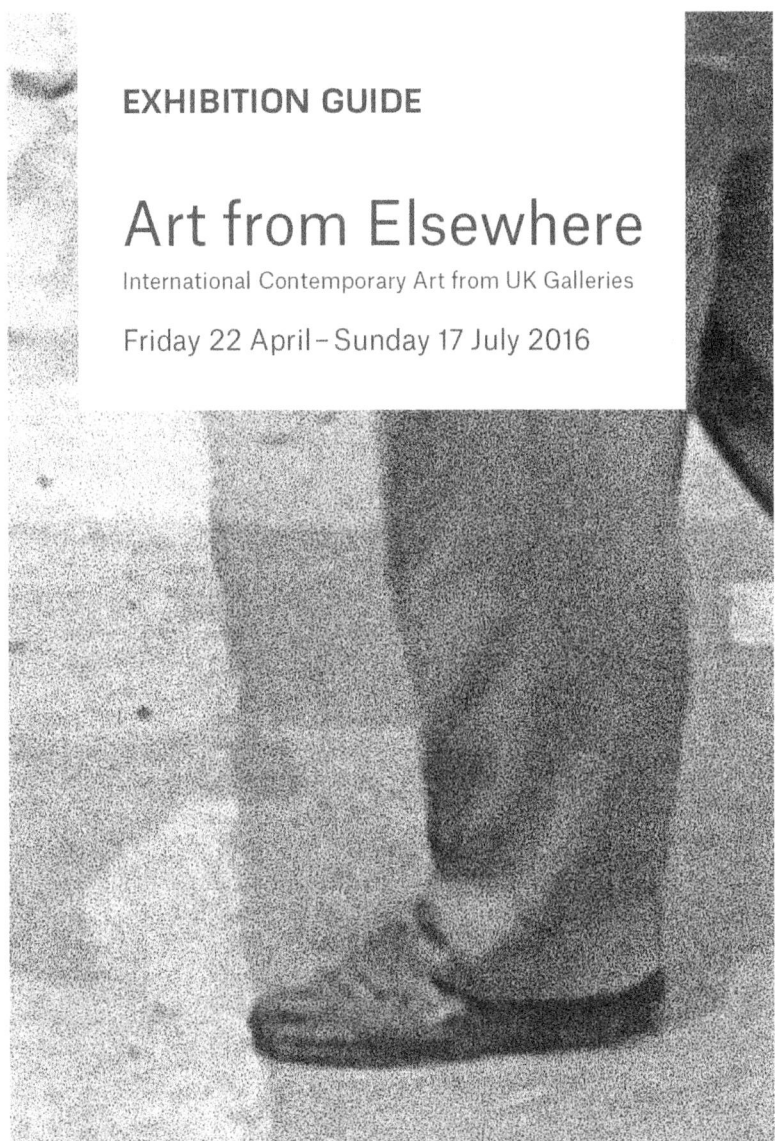

Figure 5.1 The cover of the exhibition guide for *Art from Elsewhere*
Source: © Arnolfini

suggesting that a cultural institution can be dedicated to its 'unworking' – that it can consciously sustain this openness and alterity.

This chapter draws links between Nancy's concept of 'co-appearing' and Hannah Arendt's 'space of appearance'. Arendt's writings on the 'space of appearance' – a kind of contemporary, revised *polis* – illuminate additional characteristics of 'co-appearing'. Referring to 'appearance' in texts by Nancy and Arendt, Philip Armstrong writes: 'it is in Arendt's text that the "space of appearance" becomes a critical dimension in which to think the effaced place of speech and action in our modernity' (2010: 13). Approaching Arendt's writings on the *polis* through an understanding of the *polis* as a contingent space shared *between* people – a space where shared separation characterises approaches to political engagement – the chapter explores the concrete significance of 'co-appearing'. It considers how galleries curate 'public spaces' and addresses the social responsibility inherent in institutional practices. It looks at how cultural spaces can sustain contingent 'spaces of appearance'. This section begins to outline the ethics inherent in Arendt's and Nancy's conceptualisations of 'politics' and 'the political', and what it means to question the political.

Institutions are limited by different sets of material concerns. Often, they are committed to global economic, social and political discourses that have an immediate and powerful impact on a great number of people. I argue that although they might have an apparently fixed or established identity within a cultural scene, institutions can still interact with their audiences in a way that opens up new cultural discourses outside of the establishment.

Co-appearing and the Political

As with 'spacing' and 'exscribing', 'co-appearing' is quasi-ontological – it is characterised by relationality, by shared separation. 'Co-appearing' particularly spotlights the political relevance of Nancy's thought. However, to understand co-appearing as the metaphysical process of being, rather than a concrete or determined 'thing', Nancy differentiates between 'being together' and 'togetherness'. 'Being together' is an unfolding simultaneity, an awareness of the Otherness of the other (including an awareness of the limits of this awareness itself). On the contrary, 'togetherness' refers to a defined group or collection 'in the sense of being a substantive entity . . . that is indifferent to the being together ("in common") of the objects of the collection' (BSP 2000: 60). 'To be' is 'to be together' with Others, and although this can lead to 'togetherness', Nancy emphasises the consciousness of *being* together, rather than the affiliation or identity that becomes definite. There is a sociality inherent in 'being' that is threatened when it becomes instrumentalised – the development of a function assumes fixed identities within the group, and often a fixed position of the group itself. A little later in *Being Singular Plural*, under a section that addresses 'The Spectacle of Society', Nancy reminds us that:

> If being-with is the sharing of a simultaneous space-time, then it involves a presentation of this space-time as such. In order to say 'we', one must present the 'here and now' of this 'we'. Or rather, saying 'we' brings about the presentation of a 'here and now', however it is determined: as a room, a region, a group of friends, an association, a 'people'.
>
> (BSP 2000: 65)

To identify a 'we' is to assert a tangible 'togetherness', and by focusing on this togetherness and 'using' it to achieve a preconceived goal, the 'being-together' from which it arose can become simply a symbol. On the other hand, sustained awareness of *how* we are 'we' sustains consciousness of the processes as well as the outcome. It simultaneously demands a consciousness of and withdrawal from 'togetherness' to allow for 'being together' to transcend functionalisation and allow for critical engagement with the collective ideology that has characterised the 'we'.

To acknowledge that 'being-together' differs from 'togetherness', even as the two are concurrent, therefore has social significance. When it comes to political engagement, we can begin to see that 'politics' is concerned with managing the mobilisation of already-defined groups. How then can we emphasise the 'being-together' that allows for creative and critical engagement? And why is this important?

Retreating the Political addresses these issues through an exploration of the relationship between politics and philosophy. Broadly speaking, it argues that we should not derive a politics from philosophy because this reinforces philosophy as a closed field (or a conceptual 'togetherness'). Instead, our social and political obligation is to question philosophy, so as to sustain the question of the political and retain the indeterminacy of being-together. Nancy and Lacoue-Labarthe, in their opening address to the Centre for Philosophical Research on the Political, which they founded in 1980 to explore and question the relationship between philosophy and politics, advise: 'vigilance is necessary as regards every positive discourse, that is to say as regards every discourse formed by a pretension to grasp social and political phenomena on the basis of a simple positivity – whether this be ascribed to history or to discourse itself' (RtP 1997: 109). This vigilance requires that we sustain critical thinking when we are presented with 'simple truths'. The ontological significance of being singular plural brings with it a social obligation to question universal 'truths', and to affirm the incommensurability of being. To question 'simple positivities' indicates that one retreats from, or withdraws from, an illusion of certainty or a sense that meaning is only generated through how something is fixed and mobilised.

The difference between 'individual' being-together and 'collective' being-together revolves around a shift from asking 'how do *I* appear?' to 'how do *we* appear?'. To ask 'how do I appear?' is to acknowledge individual agency and choice, dependent as this is on being singular plural. To ask 'how do we appear?' is to acknowledge the uncertain agency of co-appearing and co-operating, based as it is on individuals appearing together. In the latter, the scale of agency increases, as does the risk of forming a commensurable 'togetherness'. Responding to collective action through an idea of the collective as a homogenous togetherness reinforces that perception. Such a response fails to understand the singular plurality of 'being together' and the power that can be generated through a focus on '*being* together'. In terms of the shift between an individual retreat and a collective retreat, this emphasis on '*being* together' becomes even more significant. Increasing the scale and 'contagiousness' of critical engagement can lead to paradigm shifts, not in advancing a fixed ideology, but in deconstructing social norms.

Appearing and Co-appearing

Hannah Arendt's writings on the 'space of appearance' can help us see how a reciprocal relation between philosophy and politics can be sustained in political spaces, even whilst the creation of a tangible 'togetherness' threatens to reduce these spaces to mere symbols.

In Platonic philosophy, the *polis* is understood as a delineated state, or a 'ship of state' steered by a reigning philosopher. In *Retreating the Political*, Nancy and Lacoue-Labarthe identify the idea of the *polis* as a founding political idea in the West. They problematise it, saying: 'It is through the ideal or through the idea of the *polis*, more than anything else, that the modern epoch . . . has refastened itself to the Greek origin and finality of the West, that is to say, has tried to reassert itself as the subject of its history, and as the history of the subject' (1997: 117). The defining concept of the *polis* often situates philosophy prior to politics, a presupposition that is challenged. Although Nancy and Lacoue-Labarthe question this relation through both *Retreating the Political* and the opening of the Centre for Philosophical Research on the Political, Hannah Arendt deconstructs, reframes and revises the concept of the *polis* with emphasis on the idea of 'appearance'. Her writings reveal the social mechanisms that characterise the *polis* and begin to show that, by shifting our perception of what the *polis* actually is, we can 'renovate' the foundations of Western thought, to allow contemporary cultural structures to flourish.

Arendt reflects on the Greek *polis*, a significant political space because it could generate 'power' without the use of violence. It is this idea of generating power through 'words and persuasion and not through force and violence' (1958b: 26) that defines 'the space of appearance', a discursive place informed by, but different from, the Greek *polis*. The space of appearance forms when people gather to discuss and deliberate public issues, but at the moment that both the discussion and the deliberation ends, the space of appearance disappears. Crucially, Arendt says that it 'predates and precedes all formal constitution of the public realm and the various forms of government' (1958b: 199). This 'in-formality' or 'pre-formality' is a key characteristic of the space of appearance. It is not secondary to a political agenda; it appears whenever and 'wherever men are together in the manner of speech and action' (1958b: 199). Here Nancy's differentiation between 'being-together' and 'togetherness' has particular relevance. To be together in the manner of speech and action resonates with Nancy's 'being together' as a dynamic openness to the Other, prior to any formal constitution of a 'togetherness'. Arendt defines the space of appearance as 'the space where I appear to others as others appear to me, where men exist not merely like other living or inanimate things but make their appearance explicitly' (1958b: 198). As such, although the space of appearance is inspired by the *polis*, it revises the idea of the *polis* to focus on the relationality that constituted such a political space.

How can an exhibition such as *Art from Elsewhere* generate 'spaces of appearance'? Arnolfini is a registered charity, and at the time of this exhibition, it was funded largely by the Arts Council England and Bristol City Council. It continues to maintain a clear goal to achieve 'an ambitious, eclectic programme of visual art, performance, dance, film and music, carefully curated to appeal to a broad audience' (Arnolfini website 2020). The risk with any cultural organisation (and any curated collection of art) is that it is accessible to a limited range of people or that it assumes particular social narratives and, rather than provoking thought, can close down creative or critical engagement. As such, organisations such as Arnolfini want to make sure that they engage audiences, and facilitate informal engagement with artworks shared by diverse audiences.[6] The gallery's funding depends on this, but the underlying significance is cultural. For a long time, the Arts Council England's website opened with the question: 'Why do art and culture matter?'. The first answer it gives is that 'art and culture open our minds and stir our hearts' (Arts Council England website 2017). So whilst financial impacts are important, the focus of my analysis will be on this idea that the significance of art lies in its ability to communicate a sense of the world, and a shared experience of the absenting of sense.

In exhibitions such as *Art from Elsewhere*, which directly address political art practices within the context of globalisation, it is easy to reduce political discourses to simple narratives and to situate these narratives within reinforced cultural and geographical boundaries. The title of the exhibition – *Art from Elsewhere* – aimed to generate questions relating to the political:

> Who is the insider and who is the outsider? What is global and what is local now that we can seamlessly access stories, news and worldwide images in a click? What does 'Elsewhere' mean in relation to a constantly shifting and uncertain 'Here'?

> (AFE catalogue text)

Here we see layers of interconnections: Individual audience members relating to themselves, to the artworks, to other people within the gallery and to a wider social consciousness. These themes relate to the idea of 'appearance' in the sense of 'coming into the world, and being in the world, or existence itself' (BSP 2000: 61). But for these themes to emerge, develop and be shared by diverse audiences, the gallery needs to embody these layers of interconnectivity by 'co-appearing' and making 'their appearance explicitly' (Arendt 1958b: 198).

In this context, for Arnolfini to make their appearance 'explicit' means to demonstrate that their role is inquiring rather than didactic. But how does an institution sustain their investigatory role and ensure that audiences are aware of this? Often this is most visible through participatory events, discussions, workshops and reading groups, all of which are important elements of *Art from Elsewhere*. But this is not just a performative role – the institution also needs to 'listen' to audiences and to be open and responsive to feedback. The gallery wants to facilitate this kind of informal 'in-common' engagement, but to do this they maintain a formal process of evaluation. These evaluations also allow for greater critical consciousness of how the exhibition might seem to advance a constructed collection or narrative, and demonstrates a need to understand what this signifies to different audiences. Having regularly visited Arnolfini, I often felt that the gallery generated a discursive space that enabled people to come together to share cultural experiences and to speak and act in response to the questions highlighted by the exhibition – that it was a 'space of appearance', or contemporary *polis*. For this reason I decided to join the Learning Team as a volunteer – I wanted to learn more about the methods the gallery used to 'listen' to its audiences.

Sustaining Questioning of the Political

In 'The Compearance', Nancy draws on the writings of Marx to renew the idea of the *polis* and to consider how it designates compearance, and it is ultimately inappropriable (1992: 388). Contrary to the idea of the *polis* as a powerful ship of state, this idea of a contemporary *polis* visualises something elusive and fragile. This *polis* is characterised by a sense of risk, precarity and uncertainty. Arendt says: 'Wherever people gather together, [the space of appearance] is potentially there, but only potentially, not necessarily and not forever' (1958b: 199). As such, to initiate a space of appearance depends on an individual act of courage within a public space and an openness to uncertainty. In the context of the Arnolfini, this could be the gesture of an artist creating a work, or an individual publicly engaging with an artwork. To thoughtfully engage in an artwork demands that the viewer casts aside preconceptions and questions their firmly held opinions. This also calls into question their sense of identity.

Thinking with Arendt, we can see that identity can take two forms: '*What* we are' is our identity as defined by society – having talents or shortcomings that are judged in relation to society as a whole – and '*who* we are' refers to the *way* we do things and the way we respond to Others.[7] Arendt says that to be understood for 'who' you are requires strength and courage, because to assert this identity, and to develop it, is to put oneself in a precarious position, and to question one's opinions and beliefs. She says that we do not know who we disclose when we are in sheer human togetherness. This is because to be involved in an open discourse we must respond to the unpredictable appearance of Others, regardless of 'what' we are. In this situation, individuals become part of a communicative action that has no specific end. Accordingly, all those involved disclose themselves in a way in which intent is suspended. Here we can see that being in the space of appearance gives rise to a sense of risk and vulnerability. One cannot create, or be part of, the space of appearance if they are purposefully seeking to use the space of appearance as a platform from which to achieve personal objectives and nothing more.

As I have outlined, being-together also becomes concretised as 'a togetherness'. Nevertheless, increased awareness of co-appearance can generate concern about this concretisation – concern that triggers further questioning. Without this concern or uncertainty, 'togetherness' can generate a totalitarian logic, because if we unquestioningly remain within the realm of already-decided 'truths', we can ultimately reduce and deny incommensurability. In 'The Compearance', Nancy says that 'sharing writes itself; compearance writes itself. But this word must never give the illusion of being an "answer". It gives us – it gives *us* – a program of work' (1992: 386). As in the Greek *polis*, speaking and acting together was not an end in itself, but it generated further action within society. Here, sustaining the question of the political is of ethical importance because, rather than remaining within the realm of accepted morals, we question what *is* ethical and thereby allow for and sustain ethical consciousness.

The exhibition *Art from Elsewhere* featured a number of artists from different backgrounds. Each work shone a light on different experiences in a way that provoked reflection. In many cases, the featured artworks voiced a purposeful political message. These political messages did not carry a specific agenda, but asked us to question the political logic at play within a particular reality, and for our questioning to resonate beyond the locale of the work. As such, each visitor to the gallery is called forth as a spectator to restore the conditions of visibility and affirm the appearance of the Other, perhaps creating a space of appearance. However, this response is not a given – as Arendt explained, the space of appearance is only potentially there, and it is a temporary space. So how could Arnolfini maintain the question of the political within *Art from Elsewhere* and continue to facilitate spaces of co-appearance?

As a learning assistant, I noticed how the range of different media (e.g., paintings, photography, sculpture, video installations) in the exhibition created broad opportunities for engagement – different audience members tended to engage more with one type of media than another. As part of my role as a learning assistant, I had to use Arts Council England's evaluation model – a 'Quality Metrics' pilot scheme that is delivered through a digital platform, 'Culture Counts'. One of the evaluative processes was to undertake 'behavioural studies'. For this I had to subtly follow visitors throughout the galleries, recording the time they spent in the exhibition as a whole and comment on how they engaged with the exhibition – for example, recording whether or not they read the texts, and which works they discussed more with their friends, or which works they skimmed past. This information became symbolised by a 'ladder of engagement' that collated the visitors' behaviour into different stages: orientation, exploration, discovery and immersion. Finally, I would approach the visitor(s) and ask them to share their impression of the exhibition and what they found most and least engaging. Although I was personally interested in how an informal space of appearance might be generated within the exhibition, this process of surveillance already traced a power relation that I felt stalled the 'retreat' and masked the co-appearance of the institution. This formal observational process put the institution into a position of authority – the authority to surveil individuals without their consent – and immediately dissolved any potential space of appearance. In the next section I will go on to critique this form of measurement in more depth, but for the time being, I will temporarily suspend this critique and turn to the 'data' that emerged.

One thing that quickly became obvious was that different people became active spectators of different works, whilst having minimal engagement with other works. On the whole, a visitor would leave the exhibition having been 'immersed' in one or two pieces of work. The aesthetics of the works either attracted or discouraged visitors from becoming (apparently) fully engaged spectators. I was interested to see that those who engaged with the films often seemed to reach the 'immersion' level more perceptibly. The immersion level might be indicated by a number of different behaviours: for example, if a visitor breaks away from the group they were with to become fully absorbed in the work. Often, after being immersed in an artwork, individuals would be keen to discuss the work with me or the other gallery assistant. By situating the longest video work (*A Season Outside* [1997] by Amar Kanwar) in the final gallery space, visitors tended to leave the exhibition after engaging 'immersively' in this last artwork.

Drawing from these observations, it seemed that the diverse works and subjects within the exhibition engaged wider audiences, and even though individual visitors tended to engage with only a few works according to their personal taste, there were resonant themes throughout the exhibition as a whole. Many of the visitors I spoke with said that they found the exhibition depressing. This perhaps indicates how rather than offering 'an answer', the exhibition instead sustained the political as a question – a question that demands a programme of work.

How Politics and Philosophy 'Co-belong' in the Space of Appearance

As outlined so far, one of the key ideas in *Retreating the Political* is that philosophy should not be perceived as the *origin* of the political, but that we should recognise that philosophy and politics 'co-belong' (RtP 1997: 109). The political problem we face, they explain, is that philosophy has reached its end in contemporary politics, because 'politics' ceases to ask philosophical questions. Our social and political obligation is to question philosophy, and consequently, to retain the political as a question and to trace new articulations and sites for engagement.

Arendt believes that political action first becomes manifest in the space of appearance, and that this space immediately situates the moment of action beyond, or outside of, objective ideologies. At the very start of the *Promise of Politics* – in the opening words of the book, Arendt refers to the concept of action as 'ungraspable'. She says: 'In the moment of action, annoyingly enough, it turns out, first, that the "absolute", "that which is above" the senses – the true, good, beautiful – is not graspable, because no one knows concretely what it is' (2005: 3). She says that action is dependent on plurality, on appearing together, but that the 'first catastrophe of Western philosophy is that it ultimately wants to take control of action', and that to take control of action necessitates a unity (2005: 3). In reality, this unity can only come about by grasping and wielding the 'totalitarian logic' at the heart of the political and philosophical thought (RtP 1997: XXVIII), leading to the instrumentalisation of a 'togetherness' in line with a fixed ideology (even as this fails).

On the other hand, appearance and co-appearance initiate action, in the sense of openly responding to the other in an undetermined way. Action, in this regard, is dynamic rather than controlled. It reveals and implicates the spectator, calling the spectator into the space of appearance, and in doing so, it extends and generates further action and responsiveness. Appearance generates a sense of active responsibility and an obligation to care for the Other.

Underlining the ontological significance of this later, in *The Life of the Mind*, Arendt emphasises the shared nature of this disclosure:

> In this world which we enter, appearing from nowhere, Being and Appearing coincide. Dead matter, natural and artificial, changing and unchanging, depends on its being, that is in its appearingness, on the presence of living creatures. Nothing and nobody exists in this world who's being does not presuppose a spectator. In other words, nothing that is, insofar as it appears, exists in the singular; everything that is is meant to be perceived by somebody. . . . Plurality is the law of the earth.
>
> (1971: 19)

She is saying that we are 'of the world' not 'in' the world, because being and appearing coincide. We constitute the world as we appear. And because of this our very existence assumes and necessitates a spectator. The spectator is integral to the act of appearing, and it is called in to this space of appearance. A spectator, regardless of 'what' they are, is called to respond in a way that has not been pre-decided; in a way that is receptive to the other.

This has relevance for contemporary institutions, especially an institution like Arnolfini, whose purpose, printed on the wall of the gallery, was 'to encourage participation with contemporary art by the widest possible audience, particularly those who are disadvantaged or whose voices are excluded from mainstream culture'. As already outlined, the role of the gallery is to sustain questioning of the political. To do this, it must retreat from the limits of philosophy (from philosophical and political 'truths') and allow audiences to co-appear and enter into an 'ungraspable' moment of action. At the same time, it must choose ethical modes of engagement and receptivity that do not serve to negate this overarching purpose.

The challenge in an exhibition such as *Art from Elsewhere* is to provide enough information for audiences to 'access' the works, contextualise and engage with them, but not so much information that the work is reduced to an illustration of a political message. For example, one of the artworks in the exhibition was a piece by Beat Streuli, *Pallasades* – a video projection that records crowds of people moving through Birmingham New Street. The film is slowed down, allowing viewers to focus on individuals within the crowd. Unlike other, more obviously 'political' pieces in the exhibition, *Pallasades* is politically ambiguous. By depicting individuals that make up a mass of people, it aimed to generate a feeling of connection with those individuals. Whilst a number of visitors explained that of all the artworks in the exhibition, *Pallasades* was particularly hard to understand, others highlighted it as the work that they liked the best. In both cases, the ambiguity of the artwork and its lack of an objective message meant that it was brought up for discussion more often than other works in the exhibition. Many people experienced the appearance of this particular artwork in the gallery as 'inappropriable'.

Nevertheless, there is still a risk that the artwork can be appropriated through over-contextualisation. Here, the lack of contextualisation of the piece – the fact that there was no accompanying explanation, and it was not featured in the exhibition guide – meant that this form of appropriation was also avoided. Instead, the artwork held the attention of the viewer in its suspension of 'understanding'. In this way it carried political significance because it sustained a questioning of the political.

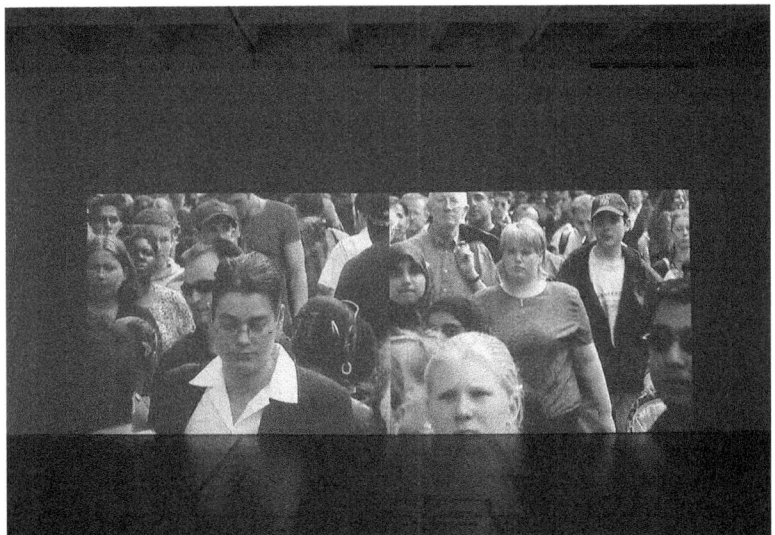

Figure 5.2 Installation view of *Pallasades* (2012) by Beat Streuli
Source: © Arnolfini

Co-appearing and Ethics

Sustaining questioning of the political carries with it an ethical imperative. In *Retreating the Political*, Nancy says:

> The commandment – and the beginning, the *archie* – of ethics has meaning only in addressing a freedom and, consequently has meaning in not *responding*, in not summoning meaning and value but on the contrary, in opening, in reopening the question – precisely the question of the end or ends of meaning.
>
> (RtP 1997: 36)

Without this re-opening of the question, political decisions become guided by assumptions and presuppositions. Co-appearing, as a condition of Nancy's ontology, brings with it an awareness that the other is also Other, and that this radical alterity is a shared condition of being. Consequently, we have an ethical imperative not to cling to assumptions of the 'fixed identities' of others. Here, ethical consciousness can only be possible through sustained questioning. Sustaining critical engagement and questioning has even greater ethical importance, because this shared questioning can sustain the freedom to challenge and reform policies and political decisions, by retracing sites in which to do this.

Up to now I have presented a rose-tinted image of Arts Council England's Quality Metrics programme – presenting it as receptive rather than prescriptive. However, looking into the brief history of the programme, it becomes immediately obvious that it carries with it a political strategy. The Culture Counts website explains that the programme began in 2011 as a 'new logic model' through which 'the cultural, social and economic value created by the arts was linked back to government policy objectives. Quality metrics were developed through extensive consultation with the cultural sector, then internationally tested and academically validated' (2017). Further reading illuminates how Culture Counts was intended as a method for quantifying and reducing cultural experiences to a set of data that could be used to 'capture the essence' of cultural participation, 'capture the quality of arts and cultural work' and to 'sense-check' the data against a preconceived idea of cultural value (Arts Council England website 2017). Here, academics are used to 'validate', rather than critically engage with, the metrics. This immediately undermines the argument that such evaluations can help an institution sustain an ethical relationship with their audiences (especially as this data is collected by unpaid volunteers who provide surveillance by sneaking around the gallery with a clipboard).

Nevertheless, this intent was challenged during the preliminary tests of the evaluation programme. Culture Counts was trialled by the Manchester consortium leading the Quality Metrics pilot and the Children and Young People External Reference Group. These pilots immediately highlighted the complexity of the participatory process, in particular the 'event' frame and 'respondent' frame. The groups testing the programme felt that there needed to be prior self-assessments, which could then be compared against peer review and participant reviews. This culminated in a 'creative intention/ reflection process . . . on both the quality of the participatory process and the performance' as reflected in the data (Arts Council England Report 2015). In turn, those who participated in the pilot programmes discussed how the data could be used to ensure a 'powerful *starting point* for conversations both within the organisation and with their participants' and the possibility of building 'algorithms and automated reporting functions that are designed to flag interesting patterns in the findings, and which should act as a natural *prompt to critical reflection and discussion*' (Arts Council England Report 2015, emphasis added).

These responses indicated that in practice, the need to 'measure the quality of participatory work' does not necessarily demand 'grading the work' or seeking to attach an exchangeable value to an artwork, but instead provides a starting point for critical discussions on how engaging an exhibition or event is. Ultimately, the meeting between members of the Manchester consortium and the Children and Young People External Reference Group suggested that the ideal outcome of this kind of research is to create a more impactful starting point for conversations and more incisive critical reflection – in other words, a sustained questioning of participatory practices. This points to a need for greater critical engagement with institutions. Whilst institutions co-appear – observe, listen and respond to their audiences – there is a need to acknowledge the inconclusive nature of what they hear and observe. This demands that they foster critical engagement with both the data and the evaluative methodologies. This feedback encourages institutions to refrain from assimilating the space of appearance, because by doing so, it begins to serve a function and can no longer be a true 'space of appearance'.

Arendt's concept of the 'space of appearance' helps us to understand the political as a discursive praxis, rather than a deployed theory. Through her focus on the *space* that is shared by (and yet separates) those who appear, she draws attention to the relationality of appearance. Reading this alongside Nancy's writings on co-appearing illuminates the ethical significance of appearance – that a lack of a specified intent and an acknowledgement of the incommensurability of the Other, is necessary in the space of appearance. Arendt acknowledges the temporality of the space of appearance – that it is only potentially there when people gather together, and that it depends on the nature of their appearance.

In the case of *Art from Elsewhere*, I am arguing that the Arts Council England's Quality Metrics scheme acted as an unethical 'logic model'. Whilst the intention behind Culture Counts was to actively engage with the political significance of cultural practices and to enable institutions to tailor their evaluations to suit the aims of the specific events and activities, the cultural, social and economic value created by the arts was linked back to government policy objectives (this was clearly stated at the time on the Culture Counts website, in a section on the background of the project that is no longer available). This aim – to link art with policy objectives – immediately clashes with the Arts Council England's principle of valuing culture because it 'opens our minds' (Arts Council England website 2017), because however benign the policy objectives might seem, they demand a reductive engagement with the image. Accordingly, any possibility for radical reorientation of ideas is immediately lost because the image is interpreted as commensurable.

The immediate feedback from the trials indicated that in practice, this objective approach to audience engagement could have potential to generate critical engagement, rather than fulfil criteria dictated by government policy (and market interests). As outlined, the group identified 'interesting patterns in the findings' but felt that these 'should act as a natural prompt to critical reflection and discussion' (Arts Council England Report 2015). In practice, the logic-model was a useful tool to generate more attentive critical engagement, but was subsidiary to the initial ethical obligation to co-appear with audiences, and to be receptive to their experiences. My first-hand experience observing audiences and discussing artworks with visitors underlined the impossibility of quantifying engagement with art, or 'capturing the quality' of the exhibition as a whole. One cannot tell what someone is thinking or feeling when they look at an artwork, and even conversations (initiated and led by learning assistants) do not indicate the 'intrinsic value' of a cultural experience. However, these studies did illuminate some patterns, and unexpected feedback triggered further conversations and responses that will impact future events and exhibitions. The fact that the gallery is undertaking these evaluations shows a willingness to develop and transform through listening to audience feedback about experiential factors, rather than simply economic statistics.

In a blog post on the Arts Council website, Simon Mellor, Executive Director of Arts and Culture, addresses the question 'Can you measure "great" art?' He explains that 'the Quality Metrics system is about enabling arts and cultural organisations to enter a structured conversation with audience members and peers about the quality of the work they are presenting' (2016). The idea of sustaining a more communicative relationship between the various and dynamic agents within the expanded field of art is encouraging. However, he goes on to say that the goal (in the next five to ten years) is to 'have a publically funded arts and cultural sector with an understanding of current and potential customers that is something akin to that already enjoyed by the commercial creative industries' (2016). This clearly showed that the priority is not to create open and receptive spaces of appearance, but rather to conceptualise the arts and cultural sector as a commercial venture in which audiences are 'customers', in turn situating art as a commensurable 'product'. As an obligatory institutional practice, it intensifies the risk of further commodification of culture, where the arts are no longer about opening our minds and stirring our hearts (Arts Council England website 2017) but about generating profitable models that serve a political ideology.

In terms of institutional practices within galleries and museums, a retreat from reinforcing the illusion of certainty inherent in 'simple positivities' requires active strategies to sustain critical discursive engagement with artworks within the institution. It requires thinking of images as sites of shared separation. Paradoxically, to renounce the 'practical realisation' of philosophical desire requires an active retreat, a carefully considered set of actions that open, rather than simplify, meaning. Cultural institutions have social responsibility. Their ethical role in allowing a retreat from the apparent certainty of our own convictions has never been more important.

In his essay 'The Free Voice of Man' in *Retreating the Political*, Nancy says that 'it is necessary *to be finished* with the demand for the production of an ethics', and later in the same essay he says that maintaining the question of the end of philosophy does not mean that 'questioning' in and of itself 'makes for an ethics of thought', but that our obligation is a 'more modest' one of '*maintaining* the *question*, as a question' (RtP 1997: 39, 40). Nancy is here critiquing normative 'ethics' but in doing so he writes of an obligation to maintain questioning – a kind of 'meta-ethical' obligation. Whilst macro-politics and globalisation are often experienced through violence and conflict, Nancy's approach to the political suggests that rather than responding directly to these acts of violence, the focus should be on countering fundamentalism, and the swing towards fundamentalism that underpins violence and conflict.

As I have argued, putting aesthetic means 'at the service' of political goals often means that creative practices are transformed into tools for larger regulatory programmes. This is not necessarily the case – Liberate Tate has a 'political goal', but it is one of radical critique rather than advocating a specific agenda that assumes a fixed political position. But within institutions, using research practices such as Culture Counts to extract intrinsic cultural values from political art practices, is *not* counter-hegemonic. Although it is possible to allow for counter-hegemonic engagement through 'listening to' and critically evaluating research practices and results, 'working with' them rather than 'using' them, this requires methodologies that resonate with these practices.

Although the Culture Counts methodologies are useful for gleaning some insights into audience engagement, they have little room for flexibility. Putting aside for a moment the troubling long-term goal of the Culture Counts programme (to create a more commercial model for cultural institutions (Mellor 2016)), the immediate intent to listen to and understand how audiences feel is often immediately blocked by the methodology of the study. The problematic nature of these methodologies is addressed in an article in *Arts Professional* in September 2016, in which editor Liz Hill offered a critique of Culture Counts: 'Arts Council to impose quantitative measures of arts quality'. In the article, she points out that, whilst the participants are reported to have 'broadly positive' responses to the idea of undertaking these evaluations, individuals spoke of the reductive nature of the research. Nevertheless, Hill explains that 'few have been willing to go on the record with their views. One unnamed NPO [National Portfolio Organisation] representative described Culture Counts as a "blunt instrument that will add cost but not a great deal of value"' (quoted by Hill 2016). The representative continues to say:

> It appears that there is a value to ACE in reducing its reliance on experienced relationship managers actually going out to carry out assessments, in favour of an automated tick box culture that will miss the nuances and surprises that are generated when you think and programme outside of the box.
>
> (quoted by Hill 2016)

These responses showed that whilst evaluation and receptivity is an important part of institutional practices, the Quality Metrics methodology and the motivations behind it are demanding a 'quantum change' in organisational attitudes to data, one that is forwarding ascriptive, reductive approaches to cultural practices.

A Summary: Co-appearing and World-forming

This chapter has further delineated the 'incline' from ontology to politics, with a greater focus on institutional practices. Again, reading Nancy in the context of institutional practices may at first seem to be contradictory, because Nancy spotlights freedom and informality rather than the stability and formality that we associate with institutions. However, I am suggesting that, rather than dismiss institutions altogether, we can begin to see how they can be devoted to 'unworking' (DC 2016: 74) and can consciously allow spaces for informal, 'non-institutional' engagement.

Awareness of the nature of consciousness and the antagonism within it can allow us to deliberately retreat from the illusion of certainty inherent in 'simple positivities' and question both individual opinions and how these might reinforce collective norms. This is a retreat that enables us to collectively retrace and renew engagement with the political. The retreat points to an ethical responsibility. Although this responsibility lies beyond possible fulfilment (in that we cannot quantify it and fully 'achieve' it), we are always relational to others because 'to be' is to be 'singular plural'. Paradoxically, this uncertain ethical responsibility is the only thing of which we can truly be certain, and our response to it characterises our collective experiences.

Through its emphasis on *re*treating, *re*tracing and *re*newing, this chapter highlights the significance of *re*composing. The prefix 're' is derived directly from Latin *re-* meaning 'again, back, anew, against' and it also carries a sense of 'undoing'. This chapter explores the idea of composing again, and composing anew. It spotlights the processual nature of recomposing – a process of re-imagining the world that diminishes and destroys the dominant image of the world as the product of capitalist ideologies, an image that often serves as a kind of sign of the inevitability of capitalism. Accordingly, this chapter leads to the idea that recomposing the image of the world sustains a sense of agency against, and in spite of, the prevalence of capitalist apparatuses.

The analysis of Arendt's writings situated institutions as agents, able to create and sustain spaces of appearance. Whilst institutions provide cultural frameworks that generate spaces of appearance, the institution is still a presence within this space. As such, institutions share in the ethical obligation of sustaining the 'appearance of disappearance' (RtP 1997: X). This can be done through questioning the political – by abstaining from didactic presentations of political art and by listening and responding to the audiences and practitioners with whom they appear. Although evaluation processes are perhaps necessary in order to listen to and engage with audiences, the results are often 'used' to fulfil preconceived policy objectives. However, I have maintained that cultural practitioners can 'work with' rather than 'use' evaluative data, by considering it as a starting point for critical engagement, rather than an exposition of 'truths'. In this way, institutions can allow for audiences to retrace the political anew.

Rather than seeking political 'truths', a fixed political 'ground' or even established political ties, art encourages us to acknowledge our own agency in maintaining a dynamic and critical relation to collective action, even as we recognise that we are always a part of it. Rather than totally rejecting institutions, our withdrawal from familiar, and often neoliberal forms of regulation within these institutions is itself a form of engagement. Because this demands an active, deliberate retreat from the illusion of certainty produced in data collection and Quality Metrics, it becomes a creative intervention. This kind of intervention is an interruption of that which is perceived as whole, or complete, and it restores our awareness of the incommensurable. Such interruptions initiate a retracing of the political. As Nancy and Lacoue-Labarthe state in *Retreating the Political*: 'such a retreat makes something appear or sets something free' and they suggest that it can impose the need for 'tracing anew the stakes of the political' (1997: 131). The retreat is the opposite of 'giving in to' or 'conceding'; it is an active and creative form of political engagement.

Notes

1. 'La Comparution', published in *Political Theory*, Vol. 20, No. 3, 1992.
2. In his book *Jean-Luc Nancy and the Thinking of Otherness: Philosophy and Powers of Existence*, Daniele Rugo explains that 'Nancy's conception of the co-essentiality of Being and Being-with opens the question of otherness at the heart of Being' (2013: 5). The idea that 'to be' is 'to be Other' characterises my approach to the idea of co-appearing. To appear with others is to be conscious of the temporality, concealment and not-knowing that is part of being (Other). For this reason, although I generally use 'the Other' and 'Others' throughout this chapter, the expression can be contextualised within this understanding of 'the other' and 'the Other' as entwined concepts.
3. Armstrong's essay explores how Nancy's understanding of appearing and co-appearing can be read as moving 'within and between a sense of displacement' – *from* appearance *to* exposure – and as 'a displacement *in* sense' (2010: 11, 12).
4. A series of essays and transcripts written and edited by Nancy and Philippe Lacoue-Labarthe.
5. Nancy's use of the term 'retreat' stems from his engagement with Derrida's concept of 'the trace' as an absent presence within language. Although Derrida's writings will not be directly explored in this chapter, they provide a point of departure for Nancy and his thinking of the retreat. The opening page of Nancy's *Retreating the Political* introduces the key terms of the book: 'retraiter' in French, which indicates a retracing and a withdrawal. The words 'retreat' and 'retrace' indicate a drawing back or the process of tracking back through previous stages to look again with close attention. Nancy and Lacoue-Labarthe address the 'retreat' with relation to the political, whilst acknowledging the polysemous nature of language.
6. A text on the wall in the entrance to the galleries says 'Our mission is to encourage participation with contemporary art by the widest possible audience, particularly those who are disadvantaged or whose voices are excluded from mainstream culture'.
7. This differentiation between 'what' and 'who' we are, is echoed by Lacoue-Labarthe, where he says 'the mutation' of the question of man from 'what is man?' to 'who is man?' is a political gesture (RtP 1997: 109).

Conclusion
Recomposing the Image of the World

Onto other possibilities of worlds. I would say that art is there every time to open the world, to open the world to itself, to its possibility of world, to its possibility thus to open meaning, while the meaning that has already been given is closed.

(Jean-Luc Nancy, 'Art Today', *Journal of Visual Culture*, 2010)

As referenced earlier, Nancy describes Covid-19 as a 'viral magnifying glass' that 'enlarges the characteristics of our contradictions and of our limitations' (13/4/2020). It is feared that the global pandemic and its economic impact could lead to a widening of social inequality and the perpetuation of prejudices. However, the magnification of social issues through our screens could also bring about a shift in how we understand the nature of our community and awareness of our roles within it. Art-making and art-viewing create a space for engagement that allows us to contemplate and respond to a changing world – it is there to 'open the world', to provide access to the world and the process of world-forming.

Focusing on contemporary art interventions and emergent creative practices, this book has explored how we might 'recompose' the image of the world. It has traced an 'incline' from ontology to the political within the writings of Jean-Luc Nancy in order to see how and why, through art practice, we can create revised images of the world. The etymology of the word 'recompose' bears layers of meaning and the sense of the word has developed throughout the book. 'Com' signifies 'with, together', and 'pose' means 'to suggest' – as in 'to pose a question' – but also carries a sense of 'questioning' or 'perplexing'. Reflecting on the task of creating an image or symbolisation, Nancy explains that this task requires 'posing the following question to each gesture, each conduct, each *habitus* and each *ethos*: How do you engage the world? How do you involve yourself with the enjoyment of the world as such, and not with the appropriation of a quantity of equivalence?' (CoW 2007c: 53). The Latin *pausare*, which brings meaning to the word 'pose', has its roots in the Greek *pauein*: to hold back, arrest, to cause to cease. In this way, 'posing' a question indicates a deferral, a holding back that can initiate a retreat. With this in mind, the word '*com*pose' indicates a sense of being *with* (com) that shares in this retreat.

Although infrequently used in English, 'recompose' therefore evokes a sense of undoing and renewing (re-) this shared 'placing' and 'questioning'. At the same time, 'recompose' acknowledges the production of a new 'composition' of the world, whilst again setting into play a renewal – a renewed attention to being singular plural that culminates in an entanglement with what cannot be clearly known, that which 'perplexes' and calls for recomposing a given image.

The aim of this book has been to explore how contemporary art intervenes in our perceptions of the world, allowing us to sustain critical engagement with the way in which we create, understand and respond to images of the world. At stake in this study is the role of visual cultures in providing a critical lens on the networks and hierarchies of power that characterise and reinforce globalisation driven by global capitalism. It has aimed to show how creative practices can create 'new forms or symbolisations' of the world.

By zooming in and spotlighting these practices and their creative potential, I hope that this book might act as a resource for theorists and practitioners. Tracing a development of theory relating to art and politics, it has explored the inherent political significance of contemporary art through embodied practices. Rather than deploying theory in practice, or assimilating practice into theory, it has developed from active reflection and participation, affirming theory and practice as indivisible.

The art practices explored in this study are still developing. In 2016, Tate announced that, from 2017, it would no longer receive sponsorship from BP. Although not acknowledged by the gallery, the Liberate Tate performers believe that we have been instrumental in this development. However, Tate has not yet fully committed to being 'fossil free' and as such, the group continues its role as a 'critical friend' and endeavours to liberate the gallery from any future ties with the fossil fuel industry.

Art Action UK has completed the ninth year of its residency, although due to Covid-19, 2020's residency, featuring Yoshio Shirakawa, was 'virtual'. It has expanded the residency to include curators and artists and is extending its research in collaboration with students at Central Saint Martins.

In 2017, Arnolfini employed a paid Visitor Experience Assistant to develop its evaluation methods in accordance with Arts Council requirements, but after some months the Arts Council support came to an end and Arnolfini paused the exhibition programme to work on a new vision for the gallery. The new exhibition programme launched in 2019 with Arnolfini as an independent charity in partnership with the University of the West of England. This partnership is now supported by Arts Council England as well as the Ashley Clinton Barker-Mills Trust.

Were there any consequences of my analysis of Nancy's 'incline' for these groups and institutions? Following my involvement in each group or organisation, I shared written reflections on my participation in each group: an essay on how Liberate Tate affects the identity of Tate, published in *Museological Review*, and an essay on the role of art after a disaster (published by Rowman and Littlefield International as part of the edited volume *artWORK: Art, Labour and Activism*). I spoke at conferences about evaluation practices within the arts. As such, I was able to further amplify the work of each group and organisation – contextualising our practices within wider discourses and extending our network of affiliations. Above all, I felt that looking at these practices in the context of Nancy's incline from ontology to the political encouraged readers and delegates to pay closer attention to nuances within these practices.

Although there is still more to explore with relation to these practices, this study will now draw together the analysis of these projects as they developed to the stage outlined earlier. Centreing on Nancy's conceptualisation of 'world-forming', I have analysed the ontological actions of 'spacing', 'exscribing' and 'co-appearing', concepts that appear throughout Nancy's writings and mark an incline from ontology to the political.

Spacing – Exscribing – Co-appearing – Recomposing

Having explored key texts and ideas within contemporary discourses on art, in particular, 'socially engaged' art, this book has focused Nancy's writings that relate to the idea of 'world-forming'. Nancy's ontology, characterised by John Paul Ricco as an 'unbecoming ontology of exposition and exposure' (2014: 86), points to the possibility that 'recomposing' is concerned with the process of 'divorcing' oneself from the ontological. Here we can begin to understand 'being' as 'spacing'. This is a kind of 'quasi-ontology' because it focuses on *the relation* between ontology and the ontic and on the 'spacing', 'distancing' and 'separating' that constitutes being. I considered how this 'quasi-ontology' leads to Nancy's post-phenomenology in which the idea of solitary subject dissolves, and 'being' is understood as a shared separation, a 'spacing'. Nancy asks his readers to think, not in terms of individuals, but of relational singularities (being singular plural).

I explored these ideas through participation in the creative activities of the art collective Liberate Tate. By interpreting Liberate Tate performances with relation to spacing, and vice versa, I looked at how identities form and transform and how ideas can become contagious. From this analysis emerged a paradoxical interpretation of art*work*. Turning to two of Nancy's texts on art, the chapter considered being singular plural with relation to art. For Nancy, the singularity of art is always 'just around the bend' (M 1996: 4). Art suspends meaning – it embodies a shared separation. Nevertheless, there is a constant inclination to find 'the meaning' of art which risks reducing or closing spaces for open, responsive and critical engagement. As such Nancy writes of a practice that is 'less unworked than devoted to its unworking' (DC 2016: 74). This devotion to unworking requires a kind of intent. However, this sense of intentionality differs from phenomenological intentionality because it is not oriented to a particular object or outcome, but towards an 'unknowing' and 'unworking'. Within the wider context of the apparatuses of global capitalism, this intentionality is needed in order to sustain spaces of freedom and the possibility of alternative ways of being.

The analysis of Liberate Tate's performances highlighted the way in which an arts group was 'dedicated to its unworking'. It looked at how Liberate Tate interrupted a cultural discourse to suspend perceptions of a cultural norm and arrest the attention of viewers. This marked the start of a process of 'recomposing' an image – in this case spotlighting BP's sponsorship of Tate and providing a critical lens that magnifies the social and political implications of fossil fuel sponsorship. The critical engagement encouraged through the group's activities recast a social norm and demanded that we 're-image' its global context. This critical engagement, characterised through 'spacing', emphasised the way in which ontology 'unbecomes', allowing for a renewal of consciousness and meaning.

I then turned to Nancy's concept of 'exscribing', an ontological concept that indicates how sense creates and exceeds materiality. Like 'spacing', exscribing manifests but withdraws from meaning. Both verbs are understood as world-forming, because they constitute reality but are beyond it. The concept of exscribing, as a motif of world-forming, was explored through participation in a series of curatorial practices for the arts collective, Art Action UK. I considered how, through becoming-present, there is also the possibility for new voices and new ideas to emerge and re-characterise the image of the world. However, as Virno points out in his book *Multitude: Between Innovation and Negation*, our consciousness is in a state of oscillation so that at any given point our sense of the world both exceeds a specific meaning and reduces meaning to predefined categories (2008: 52). For Nancy, there is ethical importance in recognising how, although we inevitably ascribe meaning, creativity and change come about through our ability to exscribe meaning and withdraw from fixed symbols of meaning.

The analysis of AAUK further developed the central term 'recomposing'. As a curatorial project, AAUK tries to 'put together' new perspectives on the 2011 disaster in Japan, and to recompose the image of these events, taking into consideration the lived experiences of artists living and working in East Japan. The word 'compose' brings with it a sense of 'to perplex'. The significance of this nuance of meaning became evident through the way in which AAUK sought to complicate simplified media narratives of the disaster and optimistic government responses.

Continuing the central analytical motif of the incline from ontology to the political, I then focused on the idea of 'the political', approaching the concept of the political through Nancy's expression 'co-appearing' and reflecting on the way in which 'retreating the political' relates to this term. I discussed the idea of 'co-appearing' alongside, and in connection with, Hannah Arendt's writings on the space of appearance. For Arendt, appearance is convergent with being – an idea that is also found in Nancy's ontology of being singular plural and his articulation of 'co-appearing'. The reason for developing this discursive analysis is to reflect on how an ontological approach to appearing has ethical and political significance, especially in the context of contemporary art.

The idea of the retreat from the political as a retreat from the illusion of certainty inherent in 'simple positivities' begins to reveal the wider significance of the ontology of being singular plural. In particular, it considered how individual perceptions are manifest in spaces of appearance and how these can either reinforce or weaken accepted social norms. Importantly, Nancy's concept of the retreat is also singular plural – through retreating we are able to critically engage with established social paradigms by retracing and renewing engagement with the political, and this happens 'with' others.

Interpreting the retreat with relation to Arendt's 'space of appearance' focused on how institutions co-appear with their audiences, exposing the shared-separation of being. Accordingly, institutions have an ethical responsibility to acknowledge the ambiguity of the Other in the space of appearance. The problem is that emergent research methodologies (in this case the Arts Council England's Quality Metrics scheme, Culture Counts) often seek to reduce cultural experiences to sets of exchangeable data – to 'capture the essence' (Arts Council England website 2017) of cultural experiences and ascribe values that link to government policy objectives. In taking part in these processes of evaluation, arts institutions risk closing down spaces of appearance and reducing the opportunity for art to generate such spaces in the first place. Despite this, evaluative processes are important ways in which institutions can listen to and communicate with audiences. Approaching these processes as ethical *praxes*, rather than a means to find an essential meaning or value in cultural practices, means that the data that is sought, and that arises, can instead be used to sustain the political as a question and to generate critical and creative engagement with visual cultures. As such, although Nancy's ontology of being-in-common is an informal relation, prior to an institution, this chapter considered the ethical importance of institutions being dedicated to their 'unworking', by sustaining spaces where this kind of informal relation (new ways of being-in-common) can develop. In this way, cultural institutions can resist the erosion of spaces of appearance.

The analysis of my role as a learning assistant at the Arnolfini and Nancy's idea of the political as a 'retreat' continued to elucidate the meaning of 'recomposing', through attention to the significance of the prefix 're-'. Nancy's use of 're-' in his terms 'retreating', 'retracing' and 'renewing' indicates how these are continual practices. The Latin *re-* means 'again, back, anew, against'. It evokes a sense of 'undoing'. As such, this prefix brings essential meaning to the term 'recomposing' because it signifies how this is an ongoing process. To advocate for recomposing the image of the world is not to encourage a one-off re-imaging; rather it is a call for a questioning and withdrawal, to continually 'open the world, to open the world to itself, to its possibility of world, to its possibility thus to open meaning, while the meaning that has already been given is closed' (Nancy 2010).

Through these considerations, I have intended to contribute to practical and theoretical approaches to political art practices. I have aimed to do so in a way that strengthens the mutuality of theory and practice. Through performance and curatorial practices, I have offered an embodied reading of Nancy's writings through three participatory roles that were undertaken not as 'formal' research that sought to establish facts or to follow a system as a detached observer, but to allow for responsive, active readings of philosophy in which theory also has creative agency. I have identified three points of 'divergence' within contemporary discussions of contemporary art:

First, through an analysis of being singular plural, the book addressed Nancy's idea of spacing to emphasise the *process* of being – as an emptying out or precipitation that occurs through the creation of finite things, and which leads to a greater sense of being singular plural. Meaning is not found 'in' finite things, but is generated through the shared force of being, even though this is necessarily linked to finite things. This idea was embodied through my participation in performances with Liberate Tate. I was able to realise this theory in practice, expand my understanding of 'spacing' through artistic performances, and to contribute to the development of further creative practices.

Therefore, the second point of divergence can be seen in the way in which this analysis differs from practices and theory that focus on the social outcome of art, on the way in which it is instrumental in creating a specific meaning, or outcome. I have argued that the functionalisation of creative practices can ultimately reduce their potential to generate social change. I have suggested that art reveals an absence of meaning. In other words, it is the *failure* of an artwork to fully 'make use' of art, that engages viewers and calls them into a process of critical reflection that embodies an ethical relation to the Other.

The third point of divergence is evident through an increased focus on the *way* in which we engage with art, as artists, curators, spectators. I have tried to develop a philosophical understanding of this engagement through Nancy's use of the term 'exscribing', calling for an 'ethos' that encourages cultural institutions and their audiences to sustain open, curious and questioning engagement with art practice, precluding 'the appropriation of a quantity of equivalence' (CoW 2007c: 53).

Developing Nancy's incline from ontology through the political within an established cultural institution, it explored how an institution can either close down or facilitate spaces of appearance – spaces in which the political is an informal discursive praxis. It suggested that institutions might 'retreat' and renew the political and, in doing so, sustain a shared space of freedom. More specifically, it emphasised how this is a *deliberate* retreat from simple positivities. This retreat can be supported though institutional practices that sustain dynamic relationships between academics, artists, activists and institutions. It can be supported through resisting neoliberal evaluation methodologies, and through critical engagement with these practices, readapting them in order to sustain, rather than close down, spaces of appearance.

In sum, this study has traced an incline from ontology to the political through a series of participatory practices. It has retraced and renewed the concept of world-forming in order to retreat from the prevailing perception that 'globalisation' and global capitalism are necessarily the same. Although capitalist systems of exchange are pervasive, continuing to emphasise general equivalence and shape each reality into a commensurable asset, world-forming can take other forms. At every moment, we collectively form the world, but at the same time there are infinite opportunities to recompose the image of the world. The process of recomposing generates critical distance from dominant apparatuses of exchange and can facilitate alternative social paradigms. This book has focused on how art practices can institute change and sustain organic, creative spaces that allow individuals and collectives to reaffirm the incommensurability of being.

Nevertheless, through this analysis, the precarity of these practices has become evident. Whilst contemporary art practices may recompose the image of the world, these images can also be recaptured by systems of exchange that reduce them to an equivalent and commensurable value.

Often, creative practices are sustainable for just a short time. Having traced the emergence and development of creative interventions, the next step is to address in more depth how such practices might develop further and how they might expand and join up with other groups and institutions to create stronger networks. In the context of this research, the next questions might be: How can Liberate Tate's success in cutting the ties between Tate and BP further expand spaces of appearance? How can Art Action UK continue to generate a critique of nuclear energy production that reaches further into mainstream discourses and connects with new audiences? How can Arnolfini retreat and retrace the political in a way that strengthens its relationships with other cultural institutions so as to become less regulated by the demands of funders?

As explained in Chapter 5, being-together and togetherness refer to two different senses of collectivity. Whilst further research might explore these practices on a wider scale, it is still important to maintain emphasis on *being*-together. How can organisations support and sustain each other in continuing to recompose the image of the world? This wider perspective, focusing on networks that operate beyond capitalist apparatuses, is the next logical step in this research project.

This book has put forward a Eurocentric reading of Nancy and arts practice. A continuation of this research project would ideally begin to map cultural networks more extensively, approaching them through a non-Western theoretical lens. Using this analysis of Nancy's writings as a springboard, further research might begin to look at alternative systems of exchange that maintain a sense of the incommensurable, and that can form dynamic connections between emergent and established cultural groups.

Bibliography

Agamben, Giorgio. (2005). *State of Exception*. Chicago: University of Chicago Press.

Andermatt, Conley Verena and Goh, Irving. (editors). (2014). *Nancy Now*. Malden, MA: Polity Press.

Appadurai, Arjun. (1996). *Modernity at Large: Cultural Dimensions in Globalization*. Minneapolis, MN: University of Minnesota Press.

Arendt, Hannah. (2005). *The Promise of Politics*. New York: Schocken Books.

Arendt, Hannah. (1971). *The Life of the Mind*. San Diego, CA: Harcourt Publishers Ltd.

Arendt, Hannah. (1958a). *The Origins of Totalitarianism*. Cleveland, OH: Meridian.

Arendt, Hannah. (1958b). *The Human Condition*. Chicago: University of Chicago Press.

Armstrong, Philip. (2010). 'From Appearance to Exposure'. *Journal of Visual Culture*. Volume 9. p. 11.

Armstrong, Philip and Smith, Jason E. (2015). 'Politics and Beyond: An Interview With Jean-Luc Nancy'. *Diacritics*. Volume 43, Number 4. pp. 90–108. Last accessed 10/18.

Arnolfini. Available at: www.arnolfini.org.uk. Last accessed 9/20.

Arnolfini Instagram. Available at: www.instagram.com/arnolfiniarts/arnolfini

Art Action UK Blog. Available at: http://artactionsupportforjapan.blogspot.co.uk. Last accessed 7/20.

Art Action UK Website. Available at: www.artactionuk.org. Last accessed 7/20.

Art not Oil. Available at: www.artnotoil.org.uk/ Last accessed 11/13–7/20.

Arts Council England. (6/2017). Available at: www.artscouncil.org.uk.. Last accessed 7/20.

Arts Council England Report. (7/2015). 'Developing Participatory Metrics'. Available at: www.artscouncil.org.uk/sites/default/files/download-file/CC_participatory_metrics_report_July_2015_FINAL.pdf. Last accessed 7/20.

Atkinson, Rebecca. (2014). 'Staying Alive; The Slippery Issue of Oil Sponsorship'. *Museums Association Website: Museums Journal*. Available at: www.museumsassociation.org/museums-journal/museums-journal-blog/05112013-staying-alive. Last accessed 7/20.

Bataille, Georges. (1998). *Georges Bataille: Essential Writings*. Edited by Michael Richardson. London: Sage Publications.

Bataille, Georges. (1997). *The Bataille Reader*. Edited by Fred Botting and Scott Wilson. Hoboken, NJ: Blackwell Publishers.

Bataille, Georges. (1988). *Inner Experience* (first published in French in 1943). Albany, NY: State University of New York Press.

Bataille, Georges. (1985). *Visions of Excess: Selected Writings: 1927–1939*. Edited by Allan Stoekl. Manchester: Manchester University Press.

Bataille, Georges. (1976). *The Accursed Share*. Volumes II and III. New York: Zone Books. Fifth edition.

Bataille, Georges. (1897–1962). *The Accursed Share: An Essay on General Economy*. Translated by Robert Hurley. New York: Zone Books. 1991 edition.

Birrell, Ross. (editor). (2007). 'Agonism, Appropriation, Anarchism'. *Art and Research Journal*. Volume 1, Number 2. Available at: www.artandresearch.org. uk/v1n2/pdfs/v1n2editorial.pdf. Last accessed 6/17.

Bishop, Claire. (2012). *Artificial Hells: Participatory Art and the Politics of Spectatorship*. Brooklyn, NY: Verso Books.

Bishop, Claire. (5/2011). 'Participation and Spectacle: Where Are We Now?' Lecture for Creative Time's *Living as Form*, Cooper Union, New York. Available at: http://dieklaumichshow.org/pdfs/Bishop.pdf. Last accessed 10/14.

Bishop, Claire. (2006). 'The Social Turn: Collaboration and Its Discontents'. *Artforum*. Volume 2, Number 6. pp. 179–185.

Blanchot, Maurice. (1986). *The Writing of the Disaster*. Lincoln, NE: University of Nebraska Press. 1995 edition.

Blanchot, Maurice. (1982). *The Space of Literature*. Lincoln, NE: University of Nebraska Press.

Boltanski, Luc and Shiapello, Eve. (2005). *The New Spirit of Capitalism*. Brooklyn, NY: Verso Books.

Bourriaud, Nicolas. (1998). *Relational Aesthetics*. Paris: Les Presse du Reel.

Bourriaud, Nicolas. (2002). *Postproduction. Culture as Screenplay: How Art Reprograms the World*: Sternberg Press

Cadava, Eduardo, Connor, Peter and Nancy, Jean-Luc. (1991). *Who Comes After the Subject?* London: Routledge.

Corkill, Edan. (18/3/2012). 'Plan to N-Shrine Reactors for Millennia'. *The Japan Times*. Available at: www.japantimes.co.jp/life/2012/03/18/general/plan-to-n-shrine-reactors-for-millennia/#.VYFx31a6Ids. Last accessed 6/17.

Critchley, Simon. (1999). 'With Being-With? Notes on Jean-Luc Nancy's Rewriting of "Being and Time"'. *Studies in Practical Philosophy*. Volume 1, Number 1. pp. 53–67.

Culture Counts. Available at: www.culturecounts.cc. Last accessed 7/20.

Davis, Heather and Turpin, Etienne. (editors). (2015). *Art in the Anthropocene: Encounters Among Aesthetics, Politics, Environments and Epistemologies*. London: Open Humanities Press.

Deleuze, Gilles and Guattari, Félix. (1983). *Anti-Oedipus: Capitalism and Schizophrenia*. New York: Continuum International Publishing Group Ltd. 1994 edition.

Deranty, Jean-Phillippe. (2013). 'The Symbolic and the Material: A Review of Jacques Rancière's "Aisthesis: Scenes from the Aesthetic Regime of Art"'. *Parrhesia*. Number 18. pp. 139–144.

Derrida, Jacques. (1976). *Of Grammatology*. Translated by Gayatri Chakravorty Spivak. Baltimore, MD: Johns Hopkins University Press

Elliott, David and Malbert, Roger. (2014). *Art from Elsewhere: International Contemporary Art From UK Galleries*. Hayward, CA: Hayward Publishing. Last accessed 2/17.

Goh, Irving. (2014). 'Sovereignty Without Subject'. *Nancy Now*. Malden, MA: Polity Press. pp. 152–170.

Grainger, Charlotte. (2019). 'Kaya Hanasaki: Shared Cultural Experiences'. *Cotonoha*. Available at: www.cotonoha.com/journal/kaya-hanasaki-shared-cultural-experiences. Last accessed 7/20.

Gratton, Peter and Marie-Eve, Morin. (editors). (2012). *Jean-Luc Nancy and Plural Thinking: Expositions of World, Ontology, Politics, and Sense*. SUNY Series in Contemporary French Thought, France. Albany, NY: State University of New York Press.

Hanasaki, Kaya. Available at: http://kayahanasaki.tumblr.com. Last accessed 7/20.

Hanasaki, Kaya. *Portrait in Mask*. Available at: http://kaya-hanasaki.tumblr.com. Last accessed 7/20.

Hardt, Michael and Negri, Antonio. (2001). *Empire*. Cambridge, MA: Harvard University Press.

Hegarty, Paul. (2000). *Georges Bataille- Core Cultural Theorist*. London: Sage Publications Ltd.

Heidegger, Martin. (1998). *Pathmarks*. Edited by William McNeill. Cambridge: Cambridge University Press.

Heidegger, Martin. (1983). *The Fundamental Concepts of Metaphysics: World, Finitude, Solitude*. Translated by William McNeill and Nicholas Walker. Bloomington, IN: Indiana University Press. 1995 edition.

Heidegger, Martin. (1978). *Basic Writings*. Edited by David Farrell Krell. London: Routledge and Kegan Paul Ltd.

Heidegger, Martin. (1962). *Being and Time*. Translated by John Macquarrie and Edward Robinson. Hoboken, NJ: Blackwell Publishers Ltd.

Hill, Liz. (16/9/2016). 'Arts Council to Impose Quantitative Measures of Arts Quality'. *Arts Professional*. Available at: www.artsprofessional.co.uk/news/arts-council-impose-quantitative-measures-arts-quality. Last accessed 7/20.

Holmes, Brian. (2001). 'Hieroglyphs of the Future: Jacques Rancière and the Aesthetics of Equality'. *Cabinet*. Issue 4. Available at: http://www.cabinetmagazine.org/issues/4/Hieroglyphs.php. Last accessed 10/14.

Holtaway, Jessica. (2/4/2015a). 'Art and Politics in East Japan: Awakening "Forgetful Spaces"'. *Art Action UK Blog*. Available at: http://artactionsupportforjapan.blogspot.co.uk/2015/04/art-and-politics-in-east-japan.html. Last accessed 7/20.

Holtaway, Jessica. (6/6/2015b). 'Post 3.11: What Can Art Do? Four Years on: Art and the Disaster'. *Art Action UK Blog*. Available at: http://artactionsupport

forjapan.blogspot.co.uk/2015/06/post-311-what-can-art-do-four-years-on.html. Last accessed 7/20.

James, Ian. (2012). *The New French Philosophy*. Malden, MA: Polity Press.

James, Ian. (2006). *The Fragmentary Demand: An Introduction to the Philosophy of Jean-Luc Nancy*. Stanford, CA: Stanford University Press.

Japan Today. (2/4/2012). 'New Safety Standards for Radioactive Cesium in Food Products Go Into Effect'. Available at: www.japantoday.com/category/national/view/new-safety-standards-for-radioactive-cesium-in-food-products-go-into-effect. Last accessed 7/20.

Jones, Jonathan. (8/9/2017). 'Is it time for the arts to start saying no to oil money?' *The Guardian*. Available at: www.theguardian.com/environment/2017/sep/08/is-it-time-for-the-arts-to-start-saying-no-to-oil-money. Last accessed 7/20.

Jones, Jonathan. (29/6/2010). 'Tate Is Right to Take BP's Money'. *The Guardian*. Available at: www.theguardian.com/culture/jonathanjonesblog/2010/jun/29/tate-bp-sponsorship. Last accessed 7/20.

Jordan, John. (3/2010). 'On Refusing to Pretend to Do Politics in a Museum'. *Art Monthly*. Volume 334. Available at: www.artmonthly.co.uk/magazine/site/article/on-refusing-to-pretend-to-do-politics-in-a-museum-by-john-jordan-2010. Last accessed 7/20.

Kellaway, Kate. (30/10/16). 'John Berger: 'If I'm a storyteller it's because I listen'. *The Guardian*. Available at: https://www.theguardian.com/books/2016/oct/30/john-berger-at-90-interview-storyteller. Last accessed 10/20.

Kester, Grant. (2011). *The One and the Many: Contemporary Collaborative Art in a Global Context*. Durham, NC: Duke University Press.

Klein, Naomi. (2014). *This Changes Everything*. London: Penguin Books.

Kohso, Sabu. (2012a). 'Radiation and Revolution'. *Borderlands E-Journal Special Issue: 'Commons Class Struggle and The World'*. Volume 11, Number 2. Available at: www.borderlands.net.au/vol11no2_2012/kohso_radiation.htm. Last accessed 7/20.

Kohso, Sabu. (3/3/2012b). 'Turbulence of Radiation and Revolution'. *Through Europe*.

Kwakkenbos, Lars. (20/1/2011). 'Art, Activism, and Permaculture'. *Foreign Policy in Focus*. Available at: https://fpif.org/art_activism_and_permaculture/. Last accessed 9/20.

Laclau, Ernesto and Mouffe, Chantal. (2014) (originally 1985). *Hegemony and Socialist Strategy: Toward a Radical Democratic Politics*. Brooklyn, NY: Verso Books.

Lacoue-Labarthe, Philippe and Nancy, Jean-Luc. (1997). *Retreating the Political*. Edited and translated by Simon Sparks. New York: Psychology Press.

Latour, Bruno. (2018). *Down to Earth: Politics in the New Climatic Regime*. Malden, MA: Polity Press.

Latour, Bruno. (2005). 'From Realpolitik to Dingpolitik or How to Make Things Public'. *Making Things Public: Atmospheres of Democracy*. Cambridge, MA: Massachusetts Institute of Technology Press.

Latour, Bruno. (2016) '*The Anthropocene and the Destruction of the Image of the Globe*'. Available at https://www.ed.ac.uk/arts-humanities-soc-sci/news-events/

lectures/gifford-lectures/archive/series-2012-2013/bruno-latour/lecture-four. Last accessed 10/20.

Latour, Bruno. (1996) (1990 in French). 'On Actor-Network Theory: A Few Clarifications Plus More Than a Few Complications'. *Soziale Welt*. Volume 47. pp. 369–381.

Lawtoo, Nidesh. (9/8/2011). 'Bataille and the Birth of the Subject'. *Angelaki*. Volume 16, Number 2. pp. 73–88.

Liberate Tate. Available at: http://liberatetate.wordpress.com/ Last accessed 11/13–7/20.

Liberate Tate Twitter Feed. Excerpt from 28/2/2014.

Mahony, Emma. (2017). 'Opening Spaces of Resistance in the Corporatized Cultural Institution: Liberate Tate and the Art Not Oil Coalition'. *Museum and Society Journal*. Volume 15, Number 2.

Martinon, Jean-Paul. (editor). (2013). *The Curatorial: A Philosophy of Curating*. London: Bloomsbury.

McBain, Sophie. (24/10/14). 'Naomi Klein: "I View Free-Market Ideology as a Cover Story for Greed"'. *New Statesman*. Available at: www.newstatesman.com/culture/2014/10/naomi-klein-i-view-free-market-ideology-cover-story-greed. Last accessed 6/17.

Meillassoux, Quentin. (2010). *After Finitude: An Essay on the Necessity of Contingency*. New York: Continuum International Publishing Group Ltd.

Mellor, Simon. (6/9/2016). 'Can You Measure "Great" Art?' *Arts Council Blog*. Available at: www.artscouncil.org.uk/blog/can-you-measure-'great'-a. Last accessed 5/17.

Michaud, Ginette. (27/4/2010). 'Outlining Art: On Jean-Luc Nancy's Trop and Le plaisir au dessin'. *Journal of Visual Culture*. 2010; Volume 9(1), pp. 77-90. doi:10.1177/1470412909354263

Morin, Marie-Eve. (2012). *Jean-Luc Nancy*. Malden, MA: Polity Press.

Mouffe, Chantal. (2013a). *Agonistics: Thinking the World Politically*. Brooklyn, NY: Verso Books.

Mouffe, Chantal. (2013b). 'Institutions as Sites of Agonistic Intervention'. *Institutional Attitudes: Instituting Art in a Flat World*. Ed. Pascal Gielen. Amsterdam: Valiz. pp. 64–74.

Nagata, Kazuaki. (3/1/2012). 'Fukushima Meltdowns Set Nuclear Energy Debate on Its Ear'. *The Japan Times*. Available at: www.japantimes.co.jp/news/2012/01/03/news/fukushima-meltdowns-set-nuclear-energy-debate-on-its-ear/#.VarR 9lYQYdt. Last accessed 7/20.

Nancy, Jean-Luc. (2016). *The Disavowed Community*. New York: Fordham University Press.

Nancy, Jean-Luc. (14/12/2015). 'The Weight of Our History'. *Critical Legal Thinking*. Available at: http://criticallegalthinking.com/2015/12/14/the-weight-of-our-history/. Last accessed 7/20.

Nancy, Jean-Luc. (2014a). *After Fukushima: The Equivalence of Catastrophes*. New York: Fordham University Press.

Nancy, Jean-Luc. (2014b). *Being Nude: The Skin of Images*. New York: Fordham University Press.

Nancy, Jean-Luc. (3/11/2011). 'What the Arab Peoples Signify to Us'. *Verso Blog*. Available at: www.versobooks.com/blogs/455-what-the-arab-peoples-signify-to-us-by-jean-luc-nancy. Last accessed 9/16. Translation of the original article in French is in *Libération* published 28 March 2011.

Nancy, Jean-Luc. (2010). 'Art Today'. *Journal of Visual Culture*. Available at: http://vcu.sagepub.com/content/9/1/91.full.pdf+html. Last accessed 7/20.

Nancy, Jean-Luc. (2008). *Dis-Enclosure: The Deconstruction of Christianity*. New York: Fordham University Press.

Nancy, Jean-Luc. (2007a). *Listening*. New York: Fordham University Press.

Nancy, Jean-Luc. (2007b). 'Nothing but the World: An Interview With Vacarme, Rethinking Marxism'. *Vacarme*. Volume 19, Number 4. pp. 521–535.

Nancy, Jean-Luc. (2007c). *The Creation of the World or Globalization*. Albany, NY: State University of New York Press.

Nancy, Jean-Luc. (2006). *Multiple Arts: The Muses II*. Stanford, CA: Stanford University Press.

Nancy, Jean-Luc. (2005). *The Ground of the Image*. New York: Fordham University Press.

Nancy, Jean-Luc. (2000). *Being Singular Plural*. Stanford, CA: Stanford University Press.

Nancy, Jean-Luc. (1997). *The Sense of the World*. Minneapolis, MN: University of Minnesota Press.

Nancy, Jean-Luc. (1996). *The Muses*. Stanford, CA: Stanford University Press.

Nancy, Jean-Luc. (1993). *The Birth to Presence*. Stanford, CA: Stanford University Press.

Nancy, Jean-Luc. (1992). 'The Compearance' ('La Comparution'). *Political Theory*. Volume 20, Number 3.

Nancy, Jean-Luc. (1991a). *The Inoperative Community*. Minneapolis, MN: University of Minnesota Press.

Nancy, Jean-Luc. (1991b). 'The Unsacrificeable'. *Yale French Studies*. Number 79; 'Literature and the Ethical Question'. pp. 20–38. Translated by Richard Livingston.

National Kyodo News Post. (15/4/2012). 'Namie to Seek Medical Fee Exemption for All Residents'. *The Japan Times*. Available at: www.japantimes.co.jp/news/2012/04/15/news/namie-to-seek-medical-fee-exemption-for-all-residents/#.VarTKVYQYdt. Last accessed 7/20.

Nordicity. (6/9/2016). 'Evaluation of Participants' Experience of the Quality Metrics National Test Phase'. Available at: www.artscouncil.org.uk/sites/default/files/download-file/Nordicity%20Evaluation%20of%20Quality%20Metrics%20trial.pdf. Last accessed 6/17.

Online Etymology Dictionary. Available at: www.etymonline.com

Penzin, Alexei. (2010). 'The Soviets of the Multitude: On Collectivity and Collective Work: An Interview With Paolo Virno'. *Meditations: Journal of the Marxist Literary Group*. Number 25. Available at: www.mediationsjournal.org/articles/the-soviets-of-the-multitude. Last accessed 6/17.

Platform. Available at: http://platformlondon.org/p-publications/artoilinfographic/ Last accessed 7/20.

Rancière, Jacques. (2013) (2011 in French). *Aisthiesis: Scenes From the Aesthetic Regime of Art*. Brooklyn, NY: Verso Books.

Rancière, Jacques. (2009). *Dissensus: On Politics and Aesthetics*. New York: Continuum International Publishing Group Ltd.

Rancière, Jacques. (2004) (2000 in French). *The Politics of Aesthetics*. New York: Continuum International Publishing Group Ltd.

Redmond, Adele. (9/9/2019). 'ACE Funds "Sustainable Future" for Bristol's Arnolfini'. *Arts Professional*. Available at: www.artsprofessional.co.uk/news/ace-funds-sustainable-future-bristols-arnolfini. Last accessed 7/20.

Ricco, John Paul. (2014). *The Decision Between Us: Art and Ethics in the Time of Scenes*. Chicago: University of Chicago Press

Rugo, Daniele. (2013). *Jean-Luc Nancy and the Thinking of Otherness: Philosophy and Powers of Existence*. Bloomsbury Studies in Continental Philosophy. London: Bloomsbury Academic.

Schmitt, Carl. (1934). *Political Theology: Four Chapters on the Concept of Sovereignty*. Chicago: University of Chicago Press. 2005 edition.

Serafini, Paula, Holtaway, Jessica and Cossu, Alberto. (editors). (2018). *Artwork: Art, Labour and Activism*. Lanham, MD: Rowman and Littlefield International.

Sjöholm, Cecilia. (2015). *Doing Aesthetics With Arendt: How to See Things*. New York: Columbia University Press.

Temelkuran, Ece. (2019). *How to Lose a Country: The 7 Steps From Democracy to Dictatorship*. London: HarperCollins Publishers.

Trowell, Jane. (2014). 'The Arts, Ethics and Sponsorship; Navigating an Environmental Path'. *Arts Council Blog*. Available at: http://blog.artscouncil.org.uk/blog/arts-council-england-blog/arts-ethics-and-sponsorship-navigating-environmental-path. Last accessed 1/14.

Virno, Paolo. (2015). *When the Word Becomes Flesh: Language and Human Nature*. Cambridge, MA: Semiotext(e) Foreign Agents Series.

Virno, Paolo. (2008). *Multitude Between Innovation and Negation*. Cambridge, MA: Semiotext(e) Foreign Agents Series.

Index

Note: Page numbers in *italics* indicate a figure on the corresponding page. Page numbers followed by 'n' indicate a note.

For Product Safety Concerns and Information please contact our EU
representative GPSR@taylorandfrancis.com
Taylor & Francis Verlag GmbH, Kaufingerstraße 24, 80331 München, Germany